Chinese Americans

by Alexandra Bandon

new
Discovery
B·O·O·K·S
New York

Maxwell Macmillan Canada
Toronto

Maxwell Macmillan International
New York   Oxford   Singapore   Sydney

ACKNOWLEDGMENT

Special thanks to the immigrants who shared their personal stories. Their names have been changed to protect their privacy.

PHOTO CREDITS

front cover: Corky Lee; front and back cover (flag photo): Richard Bachmann; The Bettmann Archive: 7, 44, 59, 65; Seattle Post-Intelligencer Collection/Museum of History and Industry: 10, 109; UPI/Bettmann Newsphotos: 12, 15, 102; Reuters/Bettmann Newsphotos: 21, 27, 52; Courtesy of Ron Chew, Wing Luke Asian Museum: 30; Robert Glick, courtesy of Chinatown History Museum, New York: 38, 86, 89; Courtesy of Rod Slemmons, Wing Luke Asian Museum: 62; Chinatown History Museum, New York: 67, 76, 105; Wing Luke Museum: 73; Pemco Webster & Stevens Collection/Museum of History and Industry: 84; Paul Calhoun, courtesy of Chinatown History Museum, New York: 96

New Discovery Books
Macmillan Publishing Company
866 Third Avenue
New York, NY 10022

Maxwell Macmillan Canada Inc.
1200 Eglinton Avenue East
Suite 200
Don Mills, Ontario M3C 3N1

Macmillan Publishing Company is part of the Maxwell Communication Group of Companies.

First edition
Printed in the United States of America

10 9 8 7 6 5 4 3 2 1

LIBRARY OF CONGRESS CATALOGING–IN–PUBLICATION DATA
Bandon, Alexandra.
Chinese Americans / by Alexandra Bandon. — 1st ed.
p. cm. — (Footsteps to America)
Includes bibliographical references.
ISBN 0–02–768149–1
1. Chinese Americans—Juvenile literature. 2. Chinese Americans—History—Juvenile literature. [1. Chinese Americans.] I. Title. II. Series.
E184.C5B187 1994
973'.04951—dc20   93-32711
Summary: A look at the history of Chinese immigration into the United States, with special emphasis on the problems facing today's Chinese and how they deal with these problems.

Contents

PART I

Before the United States

⹀ 1 ⹀

Why Do They Leave?

The Countries They Leave

Chinese Americans are immigrants or the descendants of immigrants from China. If they emigrated (leaving a country is emigrating; going to a country is immigrating) from China themselves, then they are Chinese immigrants or first-generation Chinese Americans. Their children are second-generation Chinese Americans. They are also Asian Americans, along with members of such ethnic groups as Korean Americans, Japanese Americans, Vietnamese Americans, and Filipino Americans.

Chinese Americans come to the United States from one of three countries: the People's Republic of China (mainland China), the Republic of China (Taiwan), or Hong Kong. The first is a large, semicircle-shaped country in Asia, slightly larger than the United States, whose inhabitants make up more than one-fifth of the world's population. The second is a large island off the southeast coast of Asia, with a population of just under 21 million. The third is actually not a country but a colony of Great Britain, made up of one city on several islands off the coast of the People's Republic of China, with a population of 6 million.

When books and newspapers talk about China, they usually mean only the People's Republic of China, the largest and most

Ships belonging to Britain's East India Company destroying Chinese war junks during the Opium War in 1841.

powerful of the three countries. Up until the first half of the 19th century, all three formed one country, known to the world simply as China. By 1842, Hong Kong was in the hands of Great Britain, but mainland China and the island off its southeast coast that is today the country of Taiwan were still united as the only China. It was from this country that the first Chinese Americans emigrated.

Emigrants from Guangdong

Between 1849 and 1943, virtually all the Chinese emigrants who came to the United States left from the Guangdong (Kwangtung) Province in southern China. This province, whose capital is

Guangzhou (Canton), was far from the ruling forces in the northern city of Beijing (Peking). The distance enabled people of
Guangdong to escape from a country that imposed the death penal-
ty on citizens caught trying to emigrate, a law authorized by the
heavy-handed Manchus, who had ruled China under the Qing
(Ching) dynasty since 1644. The Manchus feared that Chinese
people leaving the country would ally with those outside who
wished to overthrow the Qing dynasty. Only the notoriously rebel-
lious Chinese from far-off Guangdong could hope to escape the
horrible conditions plaguing China in the 1840s. The ban on emigration was not lifted until 1868.

A devastating series of natural disasters caused widespread
famine in Guangdong between 1833 and 1882. These conditions
coincided with a population boom, but there was no increase in
food production to feed the additional peasants. Most of the land
in China was controlled by greedy landowners who made money
growing commercial crops and who made no effort to farm new
lands and expand the food supply.

Severe government corruption and high taxation only aggravat-
ed these conditions. Rebels in Guangdong tried to throw off Manchu
rule from 1851 to 1864, but they were generally unsuccessful in gaining any control in the province. Yet the civil war was severe enough
to cause more devastation to the already-ravaged countryside. Most
of the emigrants in the mid-1800s were poor laborers who left the
rural areas in search of enough money to buy property and become
influential landowners themselves. But they needed to go outside
China to earn enough money (about $500 to $1,000) to buy land.

Though most of the emigrants were laborers, many were
merchants. Between 1839 and 1842, China fought the Opium War
over Great Britain's right to import opium, a drug made from pop-

pies, into China from India. The Chinese tried to outlaw its importation, seizing and burning 20,000 chests of the drug, valued at $6 million. Britain declared war and sent its navy to China. Britain won the war, took Hong Kong as a colony, and gained the right to govern its own trading within five important Chinese ports. Soon other Western powers, such as France, Germany, and the United States, demanded the same rights. Trading took place within Chinese territory but under the jurisdiction of the foreign merchants and governments. Chinese merchants found themselves losing money to foreigners in ports that had previously maintained strict rules controlling foreign trading. The merchants left China in search of other, more profitable places to do business.

Toward a United China

The poor conditions that pushed laborers and merchants to emigrate from Guangdong lasted through most of the 19th century. The government did little to ease the plight of the Chinese in and around Guangzhou, and foreigners still controlled trade in the major Chinese ports. Chinese industry could not compete with the Western merchants.

Then China found itself involved in two devastating wars that made it clear how weak the Qing dynasty was. In the Chinese-Japanese War of 1894-1895, the Japanese crushed the Chinese, taking Taiwan and part of southern Manchuria. The Western powers, already strong in China, took this opportunity to try to gain more concessions. By 1900, the Chinese were fed up with foreign control over their ports, trading, and territories. They formed an uprising, known as the Boxer Rebellion, to try to expel the

A Chinese American standing in front of the Kuomintang office in Seattle, ca. 1930s. Many Chinese Americans supported the Nationalist party of China in the early part of the 20th century.

Westerners from China. After 55 days, the Chinese suffered a crushing defeat, and foreign control of trading tightened.

In 1908, the empress dowager Tz'u-hsi died and the infant emperor Hsüan-t'ung (P'u-i) ascended to the throne. The weakness of this new regime gave rise to a rebellion in 1911–1912, led by Dr. Sun Yat-sen, a native of Guangzhou, educated in British Hong Kong and the United States. Sun formed the Kuomintang (Nationalist party) with the aim of ridding the country of foreign influence and putting an end to thousands of years of dynastic rule by setting up a democracy with a constitution. But when the president of the newly formed republic, Yüan Shih-k'ai, died in 1916, years of civil war between the republican nationalists and rival militarists began.

The decades from the 1890s through the 1920s were characterized by extreme political turmoil. During the years after the republic fell, warlords ruled China. The population in Guangdong kept growing, and the residents of the province continued to emigrate to escape the terrible economic conditions and unstable political climate. Many Chinese joined relatives abroad, to whom they could look for help. The stories (though often exaggerated) of the successes their kin were finding in other countries, particularly the United States, prompted more peasants and merchants from Guangdong to seek economic prosperity and political stability elsewhere.

In 1925, Sun Yat-sen died before he had a chance to reestablish a republic in China. He was succeeded by Chiang Kai-shek, who, with the help of Communist party members, reinstated the Kuomintang regime in 1928. But Chiang began to arrest and execute many of the Communists, who splintered off under the leadership of Mao Ze-dong. Again, China was plagued by internal strife as the Kuomintang tried to fight off Communist control.

Chiang was distracted from this task in 1931, however, when

the Japanese invaded Manchuria. The Manchurian Incident marked the beginning of World War II for the Chinese. Then, in 1937, the Japanese waged an all-out attack on the more populated northern provinces. The Kuomintang retreated to Chongqing (Chunking), where they joined forces with the Communists to fight off the invaders. The war with Japan was brutal and the atrocities committed by the Japanese made international headlines. By the time the Japanese surrendered in 1945, many Chinese had emigrated, fearing an all-out invasion of their nation.

China's internal strife didn't end with the expulsion of the Japanese. As soon as the invaders pulled out, China found itself embroiled in another civil war between the Kuomintang and the Communists. Between 1945 and 1949, Chiang Kai-shek desperately tried to keep control of the country from Mao Ze-dong. But

Mao Ze-dong (left) and Chiang Kai-shek (right) toast at a welcoming party for Mao in 1946. Within three years, Mao led the Communist revolution that drove Chiang's Kuomintang out of mainland China.

many Chinese saw the approach of the inevitable takeover by the Communists, who were supported by the poor, hungry, and frustrated peasants and backed financially by the Soviet Union. They fled the country by the thousands.

In 1949, Chiang and the Kuomintang retreated to Taiwan, setting up the Republic of China and claiming to be the legitimate government of China. Mao declared the Communists in control of the mainland and officially named the country the People's Republic of China.

By now, the economy of China was in shambles and Chinese money was worth next to nothing. Fearing the complete loss of wealth and property, rich Chinese desperately tried to emigrate from the People's Republic with their fortunes. In addition, former officials of the Kuomintang government left, fearing the repercussions of staying under a government they had worked hard to defeat.

The face of Chinese emigration was changing. The poor peasants who had once left China in search of work now stayed to support the government they had helped put in place. Instead, the wealthy and educated left.

Communism Under Mao Ze-dong

The wealthy Chinese continued to find reasons to emigrate as communism took hold of the country. Mao immediately undertook a cleanup campaign to rid the country of dissent, corruption, and the greed of the landowning class. Some 800,000 Chinese died in the early 1950s in Mao's ruthless crusade. But soon Mao's ruthlessness affected more than just the wealthiest Chinese.

In 1958, Mao introduced a program of rapid industrialization called the Great Leap Forward. Hoping to bring China in line with 20th-century technology and production, Mao abolished all private property and forced rural peasants to work on communes. But the production expectations for the farming peasants were so high that many moved to the cities to work in factories so that they couldn't be punished for not meeting quotas. Few were left working in agriculture and, as a result, less and less land was being farmed. China could no longer produce enough food to feed its enormous population, the highest in the world. Great famine followed, and between 20 million and 30 million people starved to death in the early 1960s.

Because the program failed so miserably, Mao lost political influence to other Party leaders. He moved to Shanghai, where he organized his supporters into the Red Guards. The Red Guards were mostly students who remained loyal to Mao and the Party and campaigned against "old ideas, old culture, old habits, and old customs." In 1966, Mao and his supporters waged what they called the Great Proletarian Cultural Revolution. He called on brigades of the Red Guards to take over schools and universities and oust anyone considered to be against the Party. Many universities in China shut down between 1966 and 1970 while these purges took place.

What Mao really did was push the Red Guards to toss out the Communist-party officials he opposed. Unfortunately, the Red Guard's revolutionary tactics included violence. Particularly in danger were the educated intellectuals, such as teachers, scientists, doctors, and scholars. Many were sent away to do menial work in desolate rural areas or to clean sewers and toilets in the cities. But millions were tortured and killed. It is estimated that

as many as one million Chinese committed suicide or were murdered during the Cultural Revolution. Hundreds of thousands more fled to the United States.

Restrictive Party Policies

In the early 1980s, China made major changes in its economic policies. Mao had died in 1976, and the Communist party had come under the control of Deng Xiaoping (Teng Hsiao-p'ing) by the late 1970s. China established diplomatic relations with the United States, which had not previously recognized the People's Republic of China. The government also admitted that Mao's programs had been a failure. China began to import Western technology in an effort to modernize industry and get the Chinese economy back on

Mao Ze-dong visiting a Chinese cooperative farm in 1962. This photograph belies the devastating famine that plagued China due to Mao's industrialization program, the Great Leap Forward.

track. By the 1980s, it looked as if conditions in China were improving and fewer people would emigrate.

But the Party has kept tight control over the lives of the Chinese, and many citizens have left in protest against restrictive social policies. Chinese citizens must get approval for many things from the Party. Artists must paint Party-approved subjects and make films in styles dictated by the government. The Party even okays marriages and policies for birth control and childbearing.

China's population is exploding. The country is currently inhabited by 1.17 billion people, or more than one-fifth of the earth's population. But the Chinese government cannot provide for many more people, so it has instituted strict population-control measures. Each couple in China is allowed only one child. Those couples who choose to have more than one child are fined sums many times their yearly salary. They are denied salary increases, job promotions, and government money for housing. They are also shunned by their peers. The government can even decide that an area has too many children of a certain age and mandate that no more children be born there for an allotted time. Consequently, many Chinese leave in protest against the one-couple–one-child policy, hoping to have large families elsewhere.

The Students

Not all Chinese emigrants leave the People's Republic in protest against government policies. Some go abroad looking for things that are greatly valued but cannot be had easily in China. One is wealth made through capitalism. Another is a superior education.

The Chinese people value education above all else. But a full education is not automatically available to every student in China. Students must take difficult tests and apply to get into high school, known as senior middle school, which they enter at the age of 16. Only one in ten Chinese actually graduates from high school. They must endure more rigorous exams to get into college. Only 30 percent of those who take the college exams pass them.

Since the 19th century, Chinese students have traveled abroad for education and for knowledge that would aid in China's westernization. Yale University graduated the first Chinese student from an American university in 1854. Since then, Chinese have acquired visas (legal permissions) to study in the United States, Britain, Canada, and other Western countries because these countries have some of the most prestigious universities and up-to-date technical knowledge in the world.

After World War II, 5,000 of China's best students, technicians, and professionals came to the United States to get the training they needed to help rebuild postwar China. They were stranded in the States when the Communists took power. After China and the United States normalized relations in the 1970s, Chinese students again came to American universities.

In 1989, however, Chinese students found themselves stranded again. Students in Beijing united in May of that year to protest the lack of freedom under Communist rule. The students wanted the Chinese people to be granted more political freedom, similar to the greater freedom they had been experiencing under Deng Xiaoping. They were particularly upset about the high levels of government corruption.

They gathered in Tiananmen Square, the seat of the Chinese government for 300 years and well-known as a place where political demonstrations had occurred in the past. The protests were

17

(continued on page 20)

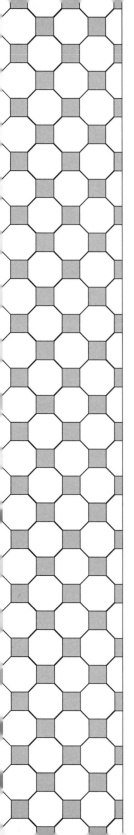

Jenny Li
Hard Work

Jenny Li is 11 years old. She lives with her mother, Xiao Lu, and two sisters, Helen (9) and Jade (6) in public housing on the Lower East Side of New York City.

We moved here from Hong Kong five years ago. My father didn't want to come, but my mother convinced him that it was better for the children to be in the United States. It has been very hard for my parents.

My father only lived with us for a short time. Now he lives out on Long Island in Southampton and works at a good restaurant. That is why he moved there. He visits us every Sunday and takes us for walks and buys us treats. He and Mother say he will move back with us soon, but I am not so sure. He makes more money where he is. I think he would rather go back to Hong Kong. Not us, though.

My mother works very hard. She is a seamstress in a huge building on Canal Street. She works from eight in the morning until seven at night, six days a week. When I grow up, I don't want to have to work like she does. She and my father work very long hours and very hard to make life better for us.

Sometimes I get tired, too. I need to study and to help with Helen and Jade. Helen and I help mother with dinner every night and we shop on Saturday for groceries. There is a lot to do. Also, mother doesn't speak English and I have to translate for her when we go out, or when she needs a prescription or something. I don't mean to complain, but sometimes I just want to play or watch TV. I like TV.

My sisters and I make lists of all the things we want. You know, clothes and records and a trip to the beach. We never show Mother, though, because she would feel bad. She always says, "My life was fated for hard work." We want her to know we appreciate what she and my father do for us.

My mother is from Guangdong in mainland China. There was a famine there, and she and her family emigrated to Hong Kong when she was my age now, eleven. In Hong Kong, she could not go to school because they were poor. She worked in a factory making plastic flowers. She doesn't want that kind of life for us. When she grew up she married my father. After Jade was born, we came to the U.S.

If my father spoke English, he could move back with us and be a waiter and make as much money as he does now. I try to teach him some words on Sundays. He seems very unhappy.

We moved to our new apartment three years ago. It is much better than our old one. My mom and I had to fill out lots of papers to get a chance to live here. And then when they said yes, we had to work one day a week to help mix cement and clean up and contribute to the housing complex. There are only 16 apartments in the building and we are lucky to have one of them. It is big and clean. We are the only Chinese people in the building. This is okay with me because I like being around different people, like in my school. But it is hard for my mother. She says she will try again to take English classes on Sunday mornings so she can learn to talk with our neighbors.

I am doing pretty well in school, but not as well as my sisters. Jade's English is perfect. I don't know yet what I want to be when I grow up. Helen says she is going to be a teacher of biology.

I wish sometimes my mother and father were together and didn't have to work so much. But I try my best to do the right things and make them happy. I got a new pair of jeans last week and Mother says I look like an American. I don't think I do yet, but maybe when I'm in high school.

peaceful, uniting many Chinese. Acrobats performed and rock bands sang, while in the foreground, thousands of dedicated protesters waged hunger strikes for the cause. By late May, the number of protesters in Tiananmen Square had reached one million.

In response to the students' demands, the Chinese government sent in the army. On June 4, 1989, 300,000 soldiers were sent to Beijing to quiet the protests. As the world watched in horror, tanks crushed the crude barricades the students had made with bicycle racks, and soldiers attacked the unarmed crowds with rifles and bayonets. As many as 1,000 people died that day.

Afterward, the Chinese government went after suspected protesters with a vengeance. Using videotapes of the demonstrations to identify the protesters, the government arrested 120,000 people. One thousand or more people were executed for their involvement. The Chinese government continues to search for more suspects. Hundreds of thousands of students were stranded abroad, 70,000 of them in the United States. Thousands more have left and continue to leave China, fearing arrest and execution.

Outside Mainland China

Thousands of immigrants come to the United States from Taiwan and Hong Kong, as well as from mainland China. Because these areas are not under the control of the People's Republic of China, the emigrants' reasons for leaving are slightly different. Yet people from Taiwan and Hong Kong are Chinese, and their immigration into the United States is considered part of Chinese immigration.

Emigrants from Taiwan leave for two main reasons: education and business. Like the Chinese from the People's Republic of

A Chinese student activist at the start of the hunger strike in Tiananmen Square, Beijing, in May 1989. Nearly one million peaceful demonstrators filled the square to protest government corruption and demand political freedom.

China, they value education highly and look to schools around the world to get the best education possible. But unlike the Communist Chinese, they have private businesses. Taiwan is a major world manufacturing center, and many emigrants use their connections in Taiwan to build successful import businesses in other countries. Others leave in search of even better economic opportunities in the United States. Emigrants from Hong Kong, on the other hand, are usually not looking for better economic opportunities abroad, unless they plan to invest some of their own money in industries in another country. Hong Kong is a center for world trade and finance and is the leading manufacturer of clothes and toys. But many Hong Kong natives are feeling pressure to leave the city soon because of the threat of losing their economic and political freedom under Chinese rule.

Britain was ceded the island of Hong Kong in 1841 but also signed a lease on the New Territories, agricultural lands on the Chinese mainland, in 1898. The lease was for 99 years and it expires in 1997. Britain and China agreed in 1984 that, when the lease on the New Territories runs out, the entire colony of Hong Kong will revert back to the People's Republic of China, under the condition that China will maintain Hong Kong's political and economic systems for another 50 years after that.

However, since the 1989 massacre at Tiananmen Square, the people of Hong Kong have feared that China will not leave the city alone for very long. Hoping to get out before the Chinese government comes in, Hong Kong natives have been fleeing by the thousands. But citizens of Hong Kong, who currently hold British passports, are not automatically guaranteed British citizenship. So the city's residents are reaching out to many countries abroad for new places to settle.

═ 2 ═

Why the United States?

The Sandalwood Mountains

hough the Chinese began to emigrate from China in the 1840s, the earliest ancestors of Chinese Americans actually arrived in Hawaii in the early 1800s, before those islands were part of the United States. Chinese traders went to Hawaii in search of sandalwood, highly prized in Chinese furniture making. They called Hawaii Tan Hsiang Shan, which means Sandalwood Mountains. Many traders stayed on the beautiful islands, marrying natives and adjusting comfortably to Hawaiian culture. But within 50 years the sandalwood supply on the islands was depleted and the trading ended.

Chinese continued to emigrate to Hawaii, however. During the 19th century, Hawaii developed huge pineapple and sugarcane industries, becoming one of the world's leading producers of these crops. The pineapple and sugar growers needed labor to tend the crops and looked to China for the manpower. Between 1853 and 1898, 46,000 Chinese came as contract laborers to work the plantations.

The Chinese were treated well by the growers. They came under a five-year contract that guaranteed free food, clothing, housing, passage to Hawaii, and between two and three dollars a month in salary. For the laborers who left China looking for a way to make money to buy land, the contract in Hawaii provided a means by which

(continued on page 26)

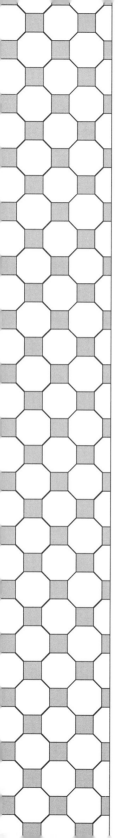

Yun Li Xiang
The Price of Freedom

Yun Li Xiang is 29 years old and lives in Washington, D.C.

I was an infectious disease doctor at one of the best hospitals in Shanghai when I decided to come to the United States. I wanted to do graduate work in bacteriology, and I was curious about life outside China. Many of my friends moved to the United States when they were in their early twenties. Some came for intellectual freedom. But most were seeking financial opportunities.

I am now a research assistant at the National Institutes of Health. To tell the truth, I do not think I will stay in research. I miss being a doctor and talking with people. If I stay in the United States, I will have to pass medical exams. I would need more schooling, not so much for knowledge, but to increase my skills in English. I still struggle with some technical language.

My husband lives in Seattle, Washington. He is a computer programmer. I married Wei Ping after I came to this country, though we met in Shanghai. His firm secured a green card for him. Now, as his wife, I, too, have one. We see each other once a month. Perhaps after my research grant is over I will move to Seattle to be with him. Perhaps not. I am a bit confused about my future right now.

Wei Ping is a good man, but he is somewhat traditional. I am very used to being on my own now. He is jealous of my friends and does not like certain things I wear, like sleeveless dresses. He thinks this is immodest. I like American dress and think it is very comfortable. And when I pierced my ears, he was very disturbed. I know these sound like small things, but they represent a new life to me. We argue a lot these days, and decisions have to be made. I am not opposed to divorce. Still, we have much in common.

My roommate here is an ABC, an American-born Chinese. Most of the Chinese I know here are ABCs. They are very different from me. They have helped me to adjust to life in this country, but they do not understand how homesick I am. Often they ask me about life in Communist China, and I tell them stories. One night I told them about the movies in China. The only time we could see American movies was in a small group. Then afterward, we would have to talk about how corrupt life in the U.S. was. I secretly enjoyed these movies. My friends cannot imagine why I am homesick for a country that makes you do crazy things like that. Still, I miss China.

One thing that helps is my dog, XuXu. She's wonderful! We can't have dogs in Shanghai because of overpopulation, so she is really a treasure to me. I send pictures of her to my parents. They say they would rather have pictures of a grandchild. I tell them they will have to wait.

One thing I like about visiting Wei Ping in Seattle is that there is a good-sized Chinese community. He is friends with other immigrants from Shanghai and with students who were at Tiananmen Square. We have such interesting conversations. We know what we have in terms of freedom in this country, but we also know what we gave up to come here.

I wonder sometimes what makes a "good life." Family and tradition are important to me, but so is being able to say and do as I want. Maybe I am becoming more and more an American woman. I am going to visit Shanghai next year and see how it feels to be back in my country.

My parents say, "Be happy, Yun Li." I think if I become a doctor again and am able to help people, maybe I will be. Do you think Americans will trust a doctor who cannot speak English as well as they do? Sometimes I wonder if people think I am stupid because I cannot speak English in a perfect way. Maybe I could practice in a Chinese community. I am a good doctor.

We will have to see. Wei Ping thinks XuXu would like Seattle. But maybe that's just his way to say he misses me.

they could save as they worked. Most of the laborers went with the intention of returning to China when their contracts were up. They thought of themselves as sojourners, or temporary residents.

But many Chinese stayed in Hawaii after their contracts expired, opening businesses such as tailor shops, shoe repair shops, bakeries, laundries, and restaurants. They built the Chinatown that still exists in Honolulu, developing a close relationship with the native Hawaiians. Today, the Chinese-American population on Hawaii is quite large. Relatives of the original farm laborers immigrated to the islands to join their families, constantly revitalizing the Chinese community. With the strong Chinese community came more Chinese eager to settle in an area where they could feel comfortable among their countrypeople.

Gold Mountain

In January of 1848, John W. Marshall discovered gold at John A. Sutter's sawmill near San Francisco, touching off one of the world's most famous gold rushes. As news spread that there was gold in California, Americans converged on the western territory, hoping to make their fortunes in the mines. At the same time, the news of the discovery was slowly making its way back to southern China through Cantonese merchants who traversed the Pacific aboard Spanish ships from Manila.

For the Chinese from Guangdong who wanted to make money and become landowners, this was good news. Soon Chinese immigrants joined the Americans swarming to California to mine for gold. When the first handful of Chinese miners returned to Hong Kong with $3,000 to $4,000 in gold dust each, the news of the

A Tiananmen protester being restrained from throwing rocks at Chinese troops. The peaceful demonstrations turned into violent riots, and the government cracked down on suspected protesters.

money to be made in Gum Shan, or Gold Mountain (the name the Chinese gave to California and the United States), spread like wildfire to Guangzhou and other parts of Guangdong. In 1851, slightly fewer than 3,000 Chinese immigrants arrived in San Francisco; by 1852, the number had jumped to 20,000.

Like the sandalwood traders who had gone to Hawaii, the Chinese in California thought of themselves as sojourners. They only intended to stay long enough to make money and return to China. But many of them never returned because they never made that money. By 1852, the prospect (surface) mining reserves were just about depleted. The Chinese were working claims abandoned long before by Americans, as newly formed mining companies began lode (underground) mining, requiring more men and machinery. Yet rumors of the wealth to be found in California mining continued to make their way to China, and immigrants continued to make their way to California.

Prospect mining continued for the Chinese as late as the 1870s, but throughout the mid-1800s, Chinese immigrants found other employment in Gold Mountain. Taking advantage of growing industry and expansion in the west, Chinese went to work in agriculture, landfill and irrigation-system construction, and transcontinental railroad construction. Not only did those already in the country take on these jobs, but Chinese "brokers" recruited more laborers from China.

In 1868, the United States and China signed a trade agreement known as the Burlingame Treaty. The treaty guaranteed the protection of Chinese nationals in the United States from discriminatory state and local laws in exchange for an end to the ban on Chinese emigration, especially to the United States. Chinese people now had the freedom to take advantage of the labor brokers.

Unfortunately for the Chinese, the United States' promises didn't last long. By the 1870s, racism in California led to many

discriminatory laws aimed at Chinese immigrants. In 1882,
Congress passed the Chinese Exclusion Act, which prohibited the
immigration of Chinese laborers. Only merchants, teachers, students, and tourists could travel to the United States. Though the
exclusion was originally meant to last only ten years, further
amendments and laws extended the immigration prohibition
against Chinese until 1943. Needless to say, Chinese immigration
to the United States dropped dramatically in the years between
1882 and 1943. In addition to the exclusion laws, racial tensions
between whites and Chinese immigrants kept many Chinese from
venturing to the Gold Mountain.

The Door Reopens

Congress lifted the ban on Chinese immigration in 1943, in
the midst of World War II. During the war, China was the United
States' ally against Japan, and supporters of Chinese exclusion
could no longer justify barring the immigration of a people whose
support was strongly needed. The government set the yearly
quota, or limit, on the number of Chinese immigrants at 105, still a
very small figure compared to other immigrant groups.

One benefit to Chinese Americans in the repeal of the
Exclusion Act was an end to the clause ordering that the federal
and state governments could not naturalize, or swear in as citizens, Chinese immigrants. At the time of the repeal, as many as
40,000 foreign-born Chinese lived in the United States. They were
now eligible to become citizens. Twelve thousand of those foreign-
born Chinese had already become eligible for citizenship by serving
in the U.S. armed forces. Many had enlisted as soon as the war

Soo Hong (Gregory) Chew and his wife, Wee Gam Har, whom he married in China in 1937. Although Chew was a United States resident, immigration restrictions kept Mrs. Chew from entering the United States until 1950.

started as a show of patriotism.

In December of 1945, after the war was over, Congress passed the War Brides Act, which allowed the wives and children of U.S. servicemen to immigrate regardless of quotas. For many Chinese Americans, this was a long-awaited opportunity. Very few women had immigrated to this country from China; usually, a husband left his wife and children in China. Many Chinese-American soldiers went to China to marry, since the ratio of Chinese women to Chinese men was very low in this country. As many as 7,000 Chinese women immigrated as war brides between 1946 and 1953.

But the War Brides Act could not assist the Chinese who worried that the struggle for power between the Kuomintang and the Communists after World War II would end in Communist rule. So Congress passed laws meant to aid those who dreaded living in Communist China. In June of 1948, when a Communist victory was imminent, Congress passed the Displaced Persons Act. The law benefited any Chinese nationals stranded in the United States by the change of power in China, including the 5,000 students and specialty workers sent for training. The 1953 Refugee Relief Act supplemented the 1948 act. Both allowed the Chinese in the United States to work indefinitely, which they were not permitted to do under their original visas, and provided political refuge for those fleeing communism at the height of the cold war.

The Floodgates Open

Even with the two laws granting relief to refugees, the number of Chinese immigrants continued to be low. It surged temporarily in 1962 when President John F. Kennedy allowed 15,000

Chinese nationals who had "mysteriously" fled to Hong Kong (probably to escape the famines brought on by the Great Leap Forward) to enter the United States as refugees. But in 1965, a new immigration law changed the face of Chinese immigration forever. The Immigration and Nationality Act of 1965 expanded quotas and eliminated discrimination by nationality in immigration.

The act, designed in part by Presidents John Kennedy and Lyndon Johnson, opened the United States to immigration from around the world. It set annual quotas for each country in the Eastern Hemisphere at 20,000, with a total limit of 170,000 for the hemisphere. Likewise, quotas in the Western Hemisphere were set at a total of 120,000, later amended to 20,000 per country.

For Chinese emigrants, the new law meant an end to long waiting lists for a place within the 105-person quota, a number that was supposed to apply to Chinese regardless of where they were born, even if they were born outside China entirely—in South America, Europe, or the like. Now each country had the same quota, and members of any race or ethnic group were eligible for the chance to immigrate. The Chinese immigrated to the United States in droves.

They came to study, to join their families, or to practice their professions. One of the provisions of the immigration act laid down a preference system detailing which reasons for immigrating were most favored by the U.S. government. At the top of the preference list were persons who had immediate family in the United States and those who had skills or practiced professions in which there were shortages here. The United States hoped to attract people with skills that could keep the United States ahead in the development of new technologies, particularly in the space industry. This meant attracting well-educated people. Since Chinese professionals from Taiwan, Hong Kong, and the People's Republic of China had excellent educational backgrounds, they were well qualified to immigrate under the preference system.

However, since the United States didn't recognize the People's Republic of China, there was only one 20,000-person quota for both Taiwan and the People's Republic. But after diplomatic relations with China opened up in 1979, the United States set aside two quotas of 20,000 people per year, one for each country. In addition, Congress expanded the quota for Hong Kong in the mid-1980s, in anticipation of the emigrants who would leave before 1997, from the 500-person quota afforded to colonies to 6,000 people a year. The United States' sizable quotas have attracted many Chinese emigrants to this country.

Immigration in the 1980s and 1990s

The expansion of the Hong Kong quota was only one of many recent changes to policies affecting Chinese immigration. Other adjustments made by Congress and the president have allowed more Chinese Americans into the country than would normally be permitted according to standard immigration laws.

Not all the Chinese immigrants to the United States qualify for visas under the preference system. In recent years, the number of undocumented immigrants from China has been growing at a steady pace. Undocumented immigrants are those immigrants who are in this country illegally, either because they stayed longer than their visas allowed or because they were smuggled into the country. Sometimes identified as illegal immigrants, they prefer to be called undocumented because, aside from the one illegal act

 (continued on page 36)

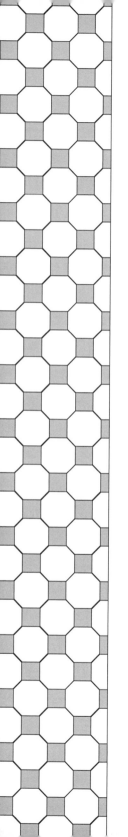

Ruby Zhang
War Bride

Ruby Zhang is 67 years old and lives near Biloxi, Mississippi.

I have many stories to tell, but the story that I like best is the war bride story. It has a happy ending, and it's about me.

My husband was a second-generation Chinese. His family lived in Mississippi in a small Delta community that had been there since the turn of the century. They owned a Chinese restaurant and served Chinese and Bayou food. My husband fought in World War II. After the war, he came to China to marry me. It was arranged through the family. The United States let war brides come into this country with their husbands. Lucky for me, my husband is a good man. I was lucky, too, because I used to dream of a faraway adventure, and not many women in China get to have their dreams come true.

In Mississippi, I adjusted very quickly. Maybe because I was young and happy with my husband and had a good mother-in-law. She liked me and welcomed me into the family. She was also happy for my help.

My husband's restaurant did not have good Chinese food because no one had been to China for so long and no one cared about cooking. I did. I found the best ingredients and knew how to cook with just the right spices. I still make the best dumplings in Mississippi. Ask my husband, Lambert; he'll tell you. To this day, we have the most popular Chinese restaurant in the Gulf—the Five Happiness.

I don't cook anymore, but I still like to decorate with beautiful pictures and paper cutouts for the different Chinese holidays. Chinese New Year is very popular at the restaurant, but Harvest Moon Festival is my favorite. I bring out pictures of Chang O, the goddess who lives on the moon, and make moon cakes like only I can. This always makes Lambert very proud. I like greeting people at the restaurant, making them feel welcome, and sometimes explaining about the holidays if they ask.

Lambert and I have three children and two grandchildren. We have been very blessed. Our oldest son and daughter both live in the northeast. David is a lawyer, an expert on import-export laws. Melissa teaches Chinese! She surprised us by wanting to study in China and learn more about our homeland. Our youngest daughter, Sharon, lives nearby. She teaches high-school math and is married to a local doctor. All our children have done well for themselves, and I think our grandchildren will, too.

When I was young and we lived in a poor village, there was a story that the old people told. The story was about a rich man who was too busy to be happy and a poor man who had time to play music and laugh. It was a long story, but you don't need to hear it all. It ended with, "money makes cares." Well, I'm an old woman now myself and I can tell you that money takes away more cares than it brings. I am happy that my children were able to go to school and study and dress in a nice manner and eat all that was good for them. I sometimes would bring flowers to a small porcelain statue I had of the God of Money. Not because I thought money was more important than love and luck and health, but because I wanted to drive that curse—money makes cares—from my heart. That was old China trying to trap me. I am an American now.

My grandchildren want to hear stories sometimes about when I was young in China. And I tell them because I like stories. But I also say, "Go make your own stories and don't think too much on the old ways." I guess I am not as Chinese in that way as you would expect. I like to look forward to the next generation. That is what I worked hard to do.

that got them into the country, they are some of the most law-abiding residents of the United States.

These undocumented immigrants do everything they possibly can to come to the United States. They want to enjoy the freedom, education, and jobs available here. Usually they are less-educated laborers, unable to meet the requirements of the strict preference system. They come to the United States for a chance to live in a society without censorship and suppression of ideas. And much like the very first Chinese immigrants, they come hoping to make their fortunes.

In 1986, in response to the growing worry over the undocumented-immigrant problem in this country, Congress passed a law granting amnesty to undocumented immigrants in the United States. Amnesty is the government's way of forgiving immigrants who have entered the country illegally. Immigrants who could prove they had lived continuously in the United States since 1981 were allowed to become legal immigrants and were given permanent resident status. With the 1986 law, Congress hoped to wipe the slate clean of its immigration problems and start anew in combating illegal immigration.

Following up the 1986 amnesty act, Congress passed another law in 1990 that set aside a whole new quota category for the immediate families of amnesty recipients. These immigrants would not be subject to the quotas imposed on relatives of other permanent residents. They also didn't have to prove "extraordinary" or "exceptional" ability to qualify for immigration.

Another change in immigration policy that affected Chinese nationals came in 1989, after the massacre in Tiananmen Square. Some 32,000 students were here on visas that would have required them to return to China for two years before changing their status to permanent resident. But the Chinese government was monitoring prodemocracy students in the United States, making it dangerous for many to return to China. In an effort to protect these students, President George Bush directed the attorney general, who oversees the Immigration and Naturalization Service (INS), not to deport (send home) any Chinese nationals against their will. He also authorized the attorney general to waive the two-year return requirement until January 1994; to assure the continued legal status of those in the United States as of June 5, 1989; and to authorize employment for the students, since those on student visas are normally not allowed to work.

Chinese immigrants from Taiwan and Hong Kong were not affected by the president's directive, of course. But other changes to immigration law did influence emigrants from these areas to choose the United States as their destination. The 1990 act that contained provisions for relatives of amnesty recipients also reworked the preference categories and, using a complicated formula, expanded the per-country quotas to a maximum of 25,650 people per year. Under the new system, preference is given to immigrants intending to invest money and create jobs in the United States. Specifically, they are expected to invest $1 million, or $500,000 in rural areas that need the industry.

This provision draws investors from Taiwan and Hong Kong in particular, since those areas can boast much successful industry. Businesspeople from Hong Kong have taken this kind of investment to other parts of the world before; Vancouver in British Columbia, Canada, is often called Hongcouver by its residents because of the number of Hong Kong immigrants who live there and own large chunks of the city's commercial property. But since the 1990 act, this kind of mass investment in booming cities has come to the United States as well, particularly to Seattle,

A Chinese-American family adapts to life in a small New York City apartment. Although many Chinese families are able to immigrate, some find that life in America is as difficult as it was in China.

Washington; Portland, Oregon; and New York City's Chinatown. In fact, real estate in some parts of New York's Chinatown has become so valuable because of Hong Kong investment that it is worth more than prime space in the World Trade Center or the extravagant Trump Tower!

Also included in the 1990 act was a provision increasing the Hong Kong quota yet again. Effective at the time the act was signed, the Hong Kong quota expanded to 10,000 immigrants per year. The act then directed that, effective October 1, 1993, Hong Kong would be treated as a separate foreign state, enabling it to qualify for the 25,650 quota on immigration each year. In addition, Hong Kong recipients of visas under this provision can wait to use them until January 1, 2002, a full five years after Hong Kong reverts back to Chinese control.

= 3 =

What Is Their Journey Like?

The Early Journeys to San Francisco

When the first Chinese immigrants traveled to California to mine for gold, it was still a crime punishable by death to leave China. The laborers from Guangdong had to be very secretive when they left, or they might be discovered, arrested, and beheaded.

The trip across the Pacific was nothing like the simple plane ride that takes less than a day now. Chinese emigrants in the 1850s traveled first by junk (a flat-bottomed sailboat) or raft across the Pearl River Delta from Guangdong to Hong Kong or Macao. From there they took an American or British steamship across the Pacific, landing in San Francisco. The trip took an average of two months, during which the Chinese chewed on lemon peels to prevent scurvy and rationed their water for tea.

Most of these early emigrants traveled on the credit ticket system. A Chinese-American association or bank would pay the passage for the emigrant—about $40 to $50 one way—as well as the cost of provisions. Once the laborer got to San Francisco, the association was required to find him employment. The total cost, often well over $100, would be deducted monthly from the laborer's paycheck after he had found a job.

Chinese immigrants landing in San Francisco in the 1800s were taken to the immigration station—a wooden shed on the waterfront. There the newly arrived immigrants would talk to a middleman who would help them arrange to send part of their wages home each month. They would also arrange through the middleman to have their bodies sent back to China in case they died. Then they would go to the section of San Francisco that was coming to be known as Chinatown to find a small room in which to live. They might also find a job in Chinatown if they didn't already intend to work in mining or railroad construction.

Immigration at the Turn of the Century

By 1903, immigration officials gave in to pressures from the Chinese-American community to build a proper receiving facility in San Francisco. They chose as the site an island in San Francisco Bay that had formerly housed a quarantine station for newly arrived immigrants with contagious diseases. Known as Angel Island, the new facility was to be the West Coast Ellis Island (the facility situated on an island near New York City through which millions of European immigrants were passing at the turn of the century). By putting the facility on an island, immigration officials hoped to keep new immigrants from communicating with relatives and associates in the city, which was a problem because many Chinese were lying, with the help of Chinese Americans living in San Francisco, to get into the country.

After the Chinese Exclusion Act took effect in 1882, the arrival process for an immigrant had become much more complicated. Arrivals from China had to prove they had the proper documentation that would allow them to enter the country legally, as merchants, teachers, students, tourists, or American-born Chinese. For most immigrants, that meant days, months, or even a year spent waiting in a detention center while officials decided if they were legitimate immigrants. The questioning an immigrant endured to prove that he was the same man named in his papers was so detailed—even down to the names of people in the immigrant's village—that as many as 30 percent of those who came in were deported for failing to give satisfactory answers.

It was no wonder the questioning was so intense. Many Chinese-American merchants took on "paper partners" to help excluded Chinese get into the country. A merchant would claim that a relative or someone from his hometown was actually his business partner, complete with a made-up name and fake papers.

After 1906, however, this ruse took on another dimension. In that year, San Francisco suffered a severe earthquake in which most of the birth and death records contained in city buildings were destroyed. Because no one could trace the existence of people supposedly born in San Francisco, many Chinese Americans claimed that they were American citizens by birth. Then they would claim they had "sons" in China, who by law would be allowed into the country regardless of exclusion.

A "paper son" memorized as much as he possibly could about his fake father, his family, and his background, and would arrive in San Francisco holding a forged birth certificate that he had bought. The immigrant and the paper father would be questioned separately, and any differences in their answers would send the immigrant straight back to China. Thousands of Chinese bypassed the exclusion laws as paper sons.

Angel Island finally opened in 1910. It was set up as a practical, strictly run detention center. Immigrants were housed in barracks with bunks in tiers of three and were expected to be in bed with doors locked and lights out by nine o'clock. For many immigrants, this was not just a temporary living situation; some were forced to stay on Angel Island for years while they patiently waited for their hearings with immigration officials. A recent campaign to restore the now-abandoned Angel Island has revealed scores of beautiful poems and drawings etched on the walls of the barracks by Chinese immigrants, describing their fears and anger about being held at the station.

The detainees on Angel Island were often women, especially after the San Francisco earthquake. Like the men who claimed paper sons, many Chinese immigrants with wives still in China pretended to be American citizens born in San Francisco. As citizens, they could sponsor their wives' immigration outside the exclusion act. Between 1907 and 1924, one-fifth of Chinese immigrants were women, compared to one-twentieth in the 1800s. But in 1924, the U.S. government passed an immigration law that included prohibitions against the immigration of people not eligible to be naturalized. Asians were not allowed to become citizens and wouldn't be until the 1940s. Thus, immigration of Chinese women was again reduced to small numbers.

Other Destinations East

As opportunities for the Chinese in California declined, mainly because of an economic depression in the 1870s and growing racism in the West, Chinese Americans looked to other parts of the country for jobs—the East Coast, the South, and the Midwest.

After the Civil War and the freeing of black slaves, many plantation owners and businessmen hoped they could find labor as inexpensive and efficient as slave labor. They also hoped to undermine the ability of the former slaves to make a living as free men and women. They looked to the Chinese.

Chinese laborers went to the Mississippi Delta, Georgia, and other parts of the South to work at cotton picking, ditch digging, railroad building, and other jobs normally held by blacks. However, they couldn't compete with the cheap, efficient labor the former slaves provided and never really established themselves as permanent workers in the South. But the arrival in the early 1870s of a few migrant workers in Mississippi was enough to start a small Chinese-American community in the Delta, which still exists today.

Chinese Americans were also hired as strikebreakers for many companies in the East, particularly in New England. Many of these immigrants moved on to East Coast cities looking for work when the strikes were over, so most of these cities had substantial Chinese populations by the turn of the century. The Chinatowns of New York, Boston, Washington, and Philadelphia were established around this time.

Immigration Since 1979

Even though exclusion ended in 1943, in the time between the Communist victory in 1949 and the establishment of diplomatic relations between China and the United States, emigration from China was fairly difficult. Except for the special refugee and war bride situations, most potential Chinese immigrants could look forward to years on a waiting list, hoping for a place in the 105-person quota. Most traveled to Hong Kong or Taiwan while they waited, which is why the 15,000 immigrants to whom President Kennedy granted relief in 1962 were from Hong Kong, not mainland China.

But when diplomatic relations opened up between the People's Republic of China and the United States in 1979, China also formally allowed its citizens to immigrate to the United States. However, the emigration process was not as easy as just boarding a plane and arriving at an American airport, free to enter the country. Foreigners who want to immigrate to the United States must first go through a lot of paperwork to get permission to do so. The Chinese must also go through a lot of paperwork to get permission to leave their country.

A person who comes to the United States must present an immigrant visa or a nonimmigrant visa upon arrival. The former is

Chinatown, San
Francisco,
around 1900

for those intending to move to the United States and become permanent residents. The latter is for temporary visitors, such as students, businesspeople, or performers. Nonimmigrant visas are very specific in stating the purpose of the foreigner's visit, down to the dates and places a musician is performing a concert or the exact place a student intends to study. The visitor cannot do any job while here except the one stated on the visa and cannot stay any longer than the visa allows. A visa is usually granted for no longer than a year and must be renewed if the holder plans to stay longer. Foreign visitors who overstay their visas are in this country illegally and can be deported.

Any Chinese getting a visa, immigrant or nonimmigrant, must apply for it at the U.S. embassy or one of its offices (consulates). There is no such embassy or consulate in Taiwan because opening relations with the People's Republic of China meant cutting them off with Taiwan. But the U.S. government bypasses this obstacle by working through the "unofficial" American Institute in Taiwan. Taiwanese Chinese can get their visas through the U.S. consulate in Hong Kong.

At the embassy the applicant shows a passport, a birth certificate, and a letter from the police confirming that he or she is not a criminal. The applicant must also pass a physical that tests for contagious diseases, such as tuberculosis.

Except for the students who come to study and end up changing their visa status, most Chinese immigrants arrive with immigrant visas. But in order to get an immigrant visa, a foreigner must qualify for one of the preference categories, either as a family member of a permanent resident or citizen of the United States or as a person with a needed talent, occupation, or skill. However, even those who qualify for one of the categories may find

45   (continued on page 49)

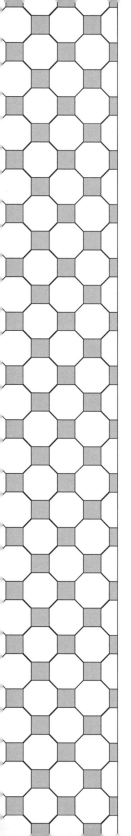

Walter Wang
Poetry in Flight

Walter Wang is 34 years old and lives in San Francisco, California. He runs a Chinese theater and is a documentary filmmaker.

My family moved to San Francisco in 1968. Before that we left the People's Republic of China for Taiwan in 1966. The trip to Taiwan was illegal, but my family had to leave to survive. My father was a professor. During the Cultural Revolution of the 1960s he was arrested. My father was a learned man. His crime was to love poetry even if it didn't praise the Communist party. He was different after being in prison—thin and bruised. He was quiet and sometimes cried for no reason. My mother made the plans to come to Taiwan. Once there, we emigrated easily to the United States.

My father fell ill of pneumonia in this country and died a year after we arrived. My mother still blames the Communists for killing her husband. My mother found work through a cousin who was a clerk in a fabric store. The two of them now own a very successful lace shop in Chinatown. My mother worked very hard and provided a good life for my sister and me. We lived in Chinatown and Mother studied English almost as hard as I did.

It was difficult at first for my sister and me. We knew no English when we moved here. I was nine and my sister seven. But we learned quickly and did well in school. My mother made sure that we studied every night. She never let us forget that we needed a good education to do well in our new country. And we have done well, more or less.

My sister teaches physics at MIT in Boston. I tease her sometimes about being a "model minority." She has always done everything right— excellent grades, scholarships. We get along well, but have different lives.

I studied film at the University of Southern California. I loved the movies as a young boy and learned English so quickly, I think, by watching them as often as I could. I stayed in Los Angeles for a while after college, making a film with some fellow students. We finished it, but it was no great success. Actually, it was pretty bad! As we say now, though, it was worth the experience.

I moved back to San Francisco, where I met Lane. She is also in film—an assistant editor. She is not Chinese. My mother has come to like her, but she is still disappointed that I didn't marry from within the community. Lane is very understanding of the situation. I am grateful for her patience and adaptability.

I work as a part-time manager of the China Palace, a movie theater in Chinatown. I like being a part of Chinatown and learning about Chinese movies. But my real work is as a documentary filmmaker. It is difficult, however, raising money to make films. I have received grants from the National Endowment for the Humanities and from various Chinese community organizations. My last film was called *Paper Sons.* It was an hour-long documentary about the men who came to San Francisco after the 1906 earthquake. The earthquake destroyed all records, so many Chinese claimed to be American citizens, and as citizens, their "sons" in China were allowed to immigrate to the U.S. Most of the "sons" who came were not blood sons, but "paper sons," young men who simply wanted to work in the U.S. Chinese culture during that time was almost all male—a bachelor society.

Making documentaries about Chinese life has been exciting, but emotionally difficult, too. My family feels so lucky to be in this country and to live lives as full as we do. Yet, when I see the prejudice and hatred so many Chinese faced coming to this country, I feel angry. Sometimes even I face this prejudice. Last week, someone yelled at me,

"Chinaman, go home." But I am home. Lane and I talk about this and wonder how it will be for our children.

I feel sometimes like I have two lives that don't quite fit together. In one life I work in the China Palace; eat in the small, delicious Chinese restaurants; walk the streets lined with herb shops and Chinese newspapers; and speak Chinese all day. Here my name is Tian Ming. In my other life, Lane and I live in Berkeley, go to films from all over the world, and have dinner with American friends where we talk about politics and art (and good restaurants!). Here my name is Walter.

I guess the point at which my life comes together is my films.

My next film is going to be dedicated to my father. Angel Island is right off San Francisco. It is a park now, and boats make daily trips for the public. However, it used to be the immigration center for Chinese emigrants in the early 1900s. They have found poems on the barracks walls written by the Chinese who were held there, sometimes for a year, waiting to get in. The poems are beautiful and speak of the anger and fear and uncertainty they experienced. I want to start my film with these poems. I want to end the film with my father's love of poetry and how that love forced us to our new home in San Francisco. It's a film about poetry and politics, and it will be called *Poetry in Flight*.

My mother is not always enthusiastic about my being a filmmaker, but she is most happy about this film. All the money for the film will come from different Chinese associations. When it is complete, I will show it in both the Chinese and American communities.

I guess you could say I am a bridge between worlds.

themselves unable to immigrate because the quota for their category is already filled. Some potential immigrants spend years on waiting lists until their names finally get to the top and are included in one year's quota.

Chinese immigrants have an added step to their emigration process. They must get permission from many Chinese government departments to leave—from their work units, from security agencies—which means filling out more applications and spending more time waiting. They are also at the mercy of local officials who review the applications and decide whether or not a person can leave.

Since the incident at Tiananmen Square, the emigration application process has become even more complicated. Right after the protests, the Chinese government announced that all potential emigrants had to reapply and get new permissions to leave. Some students found themselves being forced to confess their actions during the protest and denounce the movement before they could be considered for emigration.

However, many Chinese have complained that since Tiananmen, it is not the Chinese government that is causing the biggest hassles, but the U.S. government. After the massacre President Bush refused to relax the rules for the Chinese applying for immigrant visas. Bush, who once served as ambassador to China, feared that the Chinese government would be offended by the gesture and would stop allowing students to study in the United States. Some Chinese have noted that they went through much trouble to get all the proper permissions in China, only to be turned away by the American embassy.

Once granted an immigrant visa, a foreigner is issued a resident-alien card, commonly known as a green card. A green card is proof that an immigrant can legally stay in the United States and work, and it is the first step to becoming a citizen. A green card also entitles the holder to sponsor relatives.

Holders of green cards are required by law to carry their cards always and to report their addresses to the INS every year. It is illegal for anyone in this country to give a job to someone who isn't a citizen or doesn't carry a green card, just as it is illegal for someone without citizenship or a green card to work here. If caught, an employer of undocumented immigrants can be fined, and the immigrants themselves will be deported.

Smuggling in the Undocumented

Not every Chinese immigrant in this country has been approved for an immigrant visa. Thousands are undocumented immigrants whose journeys to the United States resemble those of the first Chinese immigrants to Gold Mountain. Coming to this country illegally today may cost an immigrant a lot of money, money he or she will pay off with many years of hard work, just as the first immigrants did when their passages were paid for by Chinese-American associations or banks. In addition, the transportation undocumented immigrants use and the journeys they endure—long, dangerous boat rides, for example—are reminiscent of the voyages taken by emigrants to Gold Mountain.

Undocumented immigrants come to the United States with the aid of smugglers. The smuggler, usually also a Chinese American, works with a network of people who arrange and carry out the entire operation. But the immigrant pays a lot of money for the help—between $10,000 and $50,000, which he or she pays off, once in this country, by a form of indentured servitude. The smugglers and their networks keep track of the immigrants and threaten them—and their families back in China—if they refuse to pay. Newspapers have reported several incidents in recent years of Chinese Americans who were severely beaten by smugglers to whom they owed money.

Some of the undocumented Chinese who are smuggled into the United States are brought in by plane, but most come by land or sea. Those who come by land come over the U.S. border from Canada or Mexico. The smugglers arrange for them to get into a South or Central American country—often Panama, for which they can easily get forged travel documents, even passports. Then they are transported over the 2,000-mile border between Mexico and the United States, which is notoriously easy to cross illegally. If they arrive in Canada first, they will probably be driven across the border with three or four others in the trunk of a car.

Those who come by sea journey for many weeks under horrible conditions. Several of the boats used by smugglers to bring undocumented Chinese immigrants to the United States have been intercepted in the last few years, and the stories the passengers told immigration agents were truly horrible.

One boatload of people, caught in December 1992, described their journey and the atrocities committed by the people transporting them. After paying $30,000 apiece to be brought to the United States, more than 150 Chinese boarded a fishing boat in Taiwan and spent 43 days at the mercy of their transporters. Food and water were strictly rationed; they had to steal from the crew just to eat. The immigrants were beaten, kicked, and threatened repeatedly by the crew. Then all 150 people were transferred to a 70-foot

American fishing vessel about 300 miles off the coast of northern California. They hid in every nook and cranny of the boat that they could possibly fit into, but a 70-foot boat is certainly not big enough to hold 150 people comfortably. When the authorities found them, they were extremely dehydrated and sick; some were in danger of dying. At least ten such boats were intercepted in 1992 alone; there's no telling how many actually made it to the United States.

On June 6, 1993, 300 Chinese caught the attention of the media nationwide when the boat attempting to smuggle them into the United States, the *Golden Venture,* ran aground on the Rockaways off Queens, New York. Ten people drowned as they tried to swim to shore, hoping to escape the authorities. The horrifying story of their journey renewed the debate over U.S. policies on policing its borders.

The people on such boats are promised jobs and homes in the

A police helicopter searches for survivors aboard the *Golden Venture.* The ship ran aground in June 1993, off the coast of New York City.

United States, but often the smugglers just leave the immigrants off to fend for themselves. Others are taken to other parts of the country by truck or van, where the smugglers place them in jobs where workers are paid low wages for long hours.

Becoming a Citizen

Chinese Americans, like other immigrants, go through a long process to become citizens of the United States. Whether they are undocumented immigrants who were granted amnesty in 1986 or legal immigrants who waited years to get a visa to come to this country, they must all take the same steps to become legal U.S. citizens.

Immigrants with green cards are entitled to apply for U.S. citizenship after they have lived in this country for five years (three years if they are married to a U.S. citizen). After filling out many long and complicated applications, the immigrant is contacted to attend a preliminary hearing at the INS. There applicants take a test showing their knowledge of U.S. government and basic history. They also show they are eligible for citizenship because they are over 18 years old and can read and write basic English. Only immigrants who are over 50 and have been here for more than 20 years can waive this last requirement.

Immigrants who pass the test have a petition for naturalization filed on their behalf. A few months later, they are contacted by the INS to be sworn in as citizens at a final hearing. They take an oath of loyalty to their new country and its Constitution. After that, they are U.S. citizens. They don't need to carry green cards or report to anyone, and they can vote, hold government jobs that require citizenship, and carry American passports.

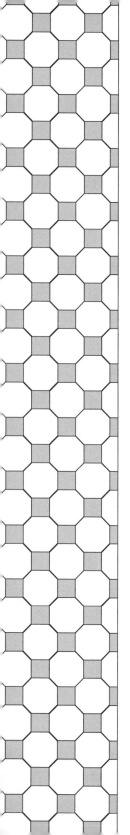

Xiao Fei Zheng
Endless Journey

Xiao Fei Zheng is 23 years old. He is an undocumented immigrant from Taiwan who lives in New York City. (Translated by Eileen Liu, Social Services worker, New York City.)

I decided to come to "the beautiful country" when I was 15. (Laughs) Do you see anything so beautiful about where I live? But that's what we called America before the journey that changed my life and my heart.

Two years ago I had finally saved enough money to pay a man who brings Chinese to America. It was a small sum, so I had to sign a contract to pay the rest once I was here and working. That boat trip was terrifying. We were all so happy when we started. We thought we would be in "the beautiful country" in 20 days. Three months later we finally made it. We picked up 120 more Chinese from a fishing boat at sea. We were crowded and without enough food. We had to wash with salt water, and I had many sores on my skin. We fought over food and water. The people who ran the boat threatened us daily. There were two huge storms, and because the boat was overcrowded, we almost sank. We thought we would die. Sometimes we wanted to.

Finally we arrived in America. We swam the final 200 yards to shore and vans picked us up and brought us to New York City. Life improved some, but not so much.

I get up at 5:00 A.M. every day to go to work for eight hours at a roofing company in Brooklyn. A truck takes seven of us and brings us back in the afternoon. Then I have to be at a restaurant here in Chinatown at 4:30 P.M. to work until 10:00 P.M.

I do this six days a week because I owe the people who brought me here much money. These people are not good people. It hurts me to say this. They are cruel and

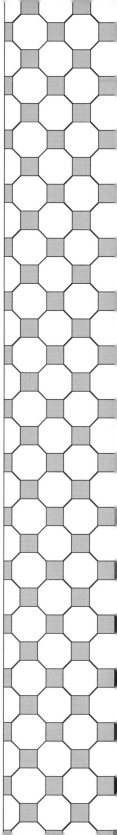

care nothing for our safety and happiness. They are my own Chinese people and remind me of the evil warlords in old China.

I live in a one-bedroom apartment with eleven other Chinese men like myself. Maybe in two more years I can pay the money and be free of this slave life.

Life is different than I planned. I thought that by now I would speak some English, but I don't know even one word. I live in Chinatown with Chinese men. I work with men who speak no English. I know there are classes, but I have no time to take them. The dreams I had in Taiwan are fading. I am so tired.

Only one good thing has happened. I met a young woman who works at the restaurant next to mine. We have met on two Sundays now and she tells me not to give up. She has been here four years and lives with her parents. She is very pretty and knows at least some words in English.

Except to go to Brooklyn to work, I have never left Chinatown. She says there is a big park in Manhattan where we can walk and we are going to go there next Sunday. I am frightened sometimes to be around Americans in their part of the city. I can't read the signs or understand what they say. But maybe the two of us together will be able to be more strong.

I don't know yet if I wished I had never come. Maybe things will turn out better than I think. But the young man who dreamed of a better life is gone. My illusions have turned to dust. I know hard things now. But I will keep trying.

PART II

In the United States

= 4 =

Prejudices and Opportunities

The Development of Prejudice

When Chinese immigrants first traveled to California, they were warmly welcomed and even encouraged to settle among the fast-growing population of the territory. In fact, they played a major role in California's statehood celebrations in 1850, parading proudly down San Francisco streets alongside other Californians. But by the 1880s, they were so strongly hated that the U.S. government passed laws to keep them out of the country.

To the miners who descended on California from 1849 to 1851, the few Chinese they encountered were polite, clean, and hardworking. They didn't see the Chinese as threatening. But when tens of thousands of Chinese began to immigrate to California, most seeking to stake gold claims, the miners looked upon the Chinese in a different light. Now they were the competition, and the miners wanted them as far away from the gold mines as possible. The miners were supported by other Californians who—ignorant of Chinese lifestyles, appearance, and language—found their new neighbors strange and often labeled them inferior.

State and local legislatures passed laws that were obviously prejudiced against Chinese Americans. Foreign miners were taxed $3 in California in 1852. Other states, such as Oregon and

A political cartoon from the late 1870s criticizing the anti-Chinese
sentiment disguised as patriotism. By 1882, this sentiment had produced
the Chinese Exclusion Act.

Washington, collected head taxes as high as $6 on Chinese and pro-
hibited these immigrants from owning mines. In 1855, California
ordered shipowners to pay $50 for each passenger who landed who
was ineligible for citizenship. According to a 1790 federal law, only
whites were eligible for citizenship, so Chinese were immediately
affected. All of these laws were passed, as their creators explained
clearly, specifically to discourage Chinese immigration.

The Chinese did not protest. It was not Chinese custom to
confront people. Instead, it was quite proper to accept one's fate,
even if that meant accepting discrimination. To avoid some of the
controversy over mining, Chinese immigrants turned to mining
claims already abandoned by whites and therefore considered by
the Americans to be useless. And because the Chinese were fairly
reserved about any criticism they had for the laws, the legislatures
continued to pile them on.

In San Francisco, the city with the highest population of
Chinese immigrants at the time, the city government passed 14
different ordinances between 1873 and 1884 that were specifically
structured to affect Chinese laundrymen. One law made it illegal
to walk on the sidewalks carrying baskets on a pole—Chinese
laundrymen carried their bundles this way. Another law placed a
tax of $15 on laundries using delivery wagons without horses, but
only $2 to $4 on those with horses; only the Chinese laundry wag-
ons were without horses. Still another ordinance required licens-
ing for all washhouses in wooden buildings, or the owners faced a
$1,000 fine and six months in jail. All of the Chinese-laundry
washhouses were in wooden buildings, but the city rejected every
license application from Chinese laundrymen. The city even tried
to pass an ordinance prohibiting queues, the long braids traditionally worn by Chinese men, but the mayor vetoed it.

One particularly devastating law required that all rooms and apartments for rent have a minimum of 500 cubic feet of space per person. Chinese Americans, usually bachelors living on low wages, tended to pool their resources and share small rooms or apartments among as many as 15 or 20 men. They lived with just a fraction of 500 cubic feet of space each and could scarcely afford to rent such large rooms for only one person.

A Different Reception in Railroad Construction

At the same time that all these laws were being enacted in California to discourage Chinese settlement in the state, Chinese Americans were finding encouragement and praise in another industry. They were actively recruited to work in building the transcontinental railroad, specifically the portion constructed by the Central Pacific Railway Company from Sacramento to Promontory Point, Utah. This portion was especially difficult and dangerous to build because it required boring huge tunnels through the granite Sierra Nevada range and laying track in the hot, dry deserts of Nevada and Utah.

When the Central Pacific was commissioned to build the railroad in 1865, it advertised for several thousand workers but received only 800 applicants. So it recruited Chinese Americans. At first the Chinese were only employed as strikebreakers, but when the railroad bosses saw how well the immigrants worked, they were kept on as full-time laborers. By the time the railroad was completed in 1869, Chinese made up 83 percent of the Central Pacific work force.

Railway workers in the 19th century. Chinese-American workers risked their lives while helping to build the main railroad lines across the United States.

Once thought to be too small and weak for the hard labor required in building the railroad, the Chinese Americans proved to be impressive laborers. Working for essentially the same wage as the white workers, but without meals included, the Chinese labored from sunup to sundown, six days a week.

Some of the most dangerous jobs they performed involved blasting with dynamite to slowly eat away at the granite mountains. Often this meant being lowered over the side of a cliff in a basket, boring a hole in which they placed dynamite, lighting a long fuse, and being quickly pulled back up the cliff before the blast. Hundreds of Chinese laborers died when they weren't pulled back fast enough or when the ropes holding the baskets broke and they tumbled down the cliffs. Others died of heat exhaustion as they struggled in the hot summers or froze to death under avalanches in the icy winters. The expression "he hasn't a Chinaman's chance" came from the work the Chinese did on the railroads, when they had a slim chance of surviving the arduous conditions of the job unhurt.

Violence against Chinese Americans

The transcontinental railroad was completed in 1869, and thousands of jubilant spectators gathered to witness the driving of the golden spike at Promontory Point. But the Chinese laborers played no part in the celebrations. Instead, they faced unemployment in the new decade, one that would be plagued by severe economic depression brought on by the Civil War. The 1870s were characterized by high prices and numerous strikes. Most Americans were having trouble finding work, and unions championing workers' rights and higher pay were gaining prominence.

The Chinese were excluded from participating in the unions. But they had little desire to join, since membership might have meant giving up chances at necessary work. Instead, Chinese Americans became notorious strikebreakers—workers brought in to replace those out on strike—in coal mining, agriculture, and in factories as far east as Beaver Falls, Pennsylvania; Bellville, New Jersey, and North Adams, Massachusetts.

This caused much resentment among those striking for better working conditions and those looking for work in bad economic times. Factory and mine owners brought Chinese workers in to avoid meeting strikers' demands. The presence of strikebreakers undermined the effectiveness of the strikes, leaving the original workers unemployed in a time without regulations for hiring and firing employees. This resentment soon turned into racial hatred, spurring protests over the immigration of Chinese laborers. They were accused of being coolies, a term used to describe indentured servants imported from China into the Caribbean to undermine the wages of former black slaves.

Most of this anti-Chinese feeling was centered in California, still the state with by far the largest population of Chinese Americans. It was also the state with the worst history of discrimination and violence against Chinese. Chinese miners had consistently been beaten or murdered in efforts to push them off successful gold claims in the 1850s and 1860s. Laws prohibiting nonwhites from testifying against whites had prevented Chinese from receiving justice in both criminal and civil court cases. When state law was rewritten in 1863 to allow African Americans, who had similarly been prohibited, to testify in such cases, the ban on Chinese testimony was specifically written into the penal code. The law was not repealed until 1872, when the Fourteenth Amendment to the Constitution made such legislation illegal.

By the 1870s the economy of California was so bad that the anti-Chinese movement was quite strong. In 1871, white residents of Los Angeles gathered to watch a policeman trying to stop fighting between two groups of Chinese Americans. Shots rang out, and one of the white observers was killed, supposedly by a Chinese immigrant. The crowd rioted and looted, attacking Chinese in their homes, beating them, and lynching many. Others died when the mob threw burning embers into their homes from the roofs, setting them on fire. Twenty-one Chinese died in the rioting and scores of others were beaten and robbed. Only eight of the rioters were convicted of crimes related to the incident; they were all out of jail within a year.

Violence against Chinese intensified in the next few years. A riot in 1877 in Chico, California, a mining town with a substantial Chinese population, led to the murder of four Chinese people. They died when they were tied up, doused with fuel, and set on fire by members of a white-supremacist organization. Another riot in 1880 in Denver killed one Chinese American, injured many others, and damaged much Chinese property.

Probably the most famous of the acts of violence against Chinese occurred in 1885 in Rock Springs, Wyoming. There, striking coal miners became violent when their Chinese co-workers

An 1885 engraving entitled "The Massacre of the Chinese at Rock Springs, Wyoming." By the 1870s and 1880s, violence against Chinese Americans was rampant.

refused to join their walkout. They attacked the Chinese, shooting at the unarmed immigrants and setting fire to their homes. They robbed many Chinese before beating them, and they threw the bodies of dead as well as live Chinese Americans onto the burning shacks. Twenty-eight Chinese died and 15 were injured. Federal troops had to be called in to protect those who escaped and to escort them back to the coal mines, but they had already lost all of their possessions. The coal company donated food and clothes, and the government set aside $150,000 to help the Chinese Americans get back on their feet.

Movements to push Chinese out of various communities spread throughout the West, continuing well into the 1880s. Anti-Chinese mobs tried to force Chinese Americans out of settlements in Idaho, Colorado, Oregon, Montana, Washington, and California. The Anti-Chinese Congress was formed in Seattle in 1885; it demanded that the Chinese leave Tacoma and Seattle by November 1 of that year. When the Chinese refused, large mobs made two attempts during the next year to gather them and forcibly oust them from the towns. One attempt included bringing them to the docks and ordering them to board a ship destined for China. Similar expulsion attempts continued into the 1890s.

Exclusion

While violence against Chinese Americans was shattering hundreds of lives in the late 1800s, another form of discrimination affected even more Chinese—those who were not allowed to come to the United States. In 1882, Congress passed the Chinese Exclusion Act, which prohibited the immigration of

Chinese laborers. Only a select few classifications of immigrants were accepted for entry into the country.

The law established exclusion of laborers for a period of ten years. Shipowners who brought Chinese laborers to the country were subject to fines of as much as $500 and a one-year jail sentence. Any laborer already in the United States who wanted to leave the country had to get proper certification or he would not be allowed back in. In addition, the law specifically forbade state and federal courts to naturalize any Chinese, reaffirming that only whites and African Americans were eligible for citizenship. An amendment to the act in 1884 reestablished the ten-year ban, extending it to 1894; more closely detailed the sections of the law that specified procedures for leaving and returning to the country; and defined *laborer* and *merchant*.

The Chinese Exclusion Act was passed at the height of

A Chinese merchant's family in New York City, ca. 1900. Because of the exclusion laws, only Chinese merchants, teachers, students, and tourists could enter the country legally after 1882.

European immigration to the United States. Chinese immigrants constituted only a fraction of the millions of immigrants who came to this country in the 19th century. Clearly, the act was a show of racial prejudice against Asians, particularly Chinese. The result was an enormous drop in Chinese immigration—as expected—as well as a large departure of Chinese already in the country. Those who remained withdrew into close-knit Chinese-American societies, avoiding contact with white Americans as much as possible.

By the late 1880s, however, immigration officials realized that an unusually large number of Chinese teachers, students, and tourists were traveling to the United States. Obviously, excluded laborers were gaining entry by passing as permitted immigrants. In addition, it was speculated that smuggling of undocumented Chinese immigrants from Mexico and Canada had begun. Anti-Chinese factions pushed for stricter controls.

In 1888, under threats that the Qing government wouldn't ratify a new treaty prohibiting Chinese laborers from emigrating, Congress pushed through the Scott Act. The law barred Chinese laborers who left the United States from returning. President Grover Cleveland, who signed the bill, declared Chinese immigrants to be "an element ignorant of our Constitution and laws, impossible of assimilation with our people, and dangerous to our peace and welfare." An estimated 20,000 Chinese laborers who had gone back to China to visit family, including about 600 who were en route somewhere in the middle of the Pacific Ocean, were now stranded, even though they had the proper certifications for reentry.

In 1892, Congress passed the Geary Act, requiring all alien laborers left in the country to register with the government. But the act further allowed that anyone caught laboring who was not able to prove that he had registered or didn't need to register

would be deported. Many American-born Chinese probably found
themselves packed up and shipped off to China for lack of convinc-
ing evidence of their citizenship. The Geary Act also extended
exclusion an additional 10 years.

From the beginning of exclusion, opponents of the laws took
their cases to court. The California courts had a history of favoring
immigrants. The federal circuit court had ruled that many of the discriminatory ordinances in California were unconstitutional, including
the one that kept noncitizens from owning property. In handling
immigration appeals, the court had almost always ruled in favor of the
immigrants, allowing excluded Chinese to enter the country. But in
1893, opposition to the Geary Act made it all the way to the Supreme
Court. The Court ruled in favor of the discriminatory acts, saying, "It
is not within the province of the judiciary to order that foreigners . . .
shall be permitted to enter," and concluding that Congress's power to
pass exclusionary immigration laws was "an inherent and inalienable
right of every sovereign and independent nation."

Exclusion, at the urging of President Theodore Roosevelt,
was again extended in 1902. Finally, in 1904, the prohibition
against Chinese laborer immigration was continued indefinitely.
Chinese Americans claimed one victory in 1905, however.
Responding to a long string of discriminatory laws and practices
by the U.S. government, Chinese Americans sent telegrams to the
Chinese foreign ministry calling for a boycott by Chinese merchants of American goods. Merchants in central and south China
complied, refusing to do business with Americans and canceling
orders from the United States. The boycott lasted only a year and
did little damage to the U.S. economy, but it effectively halted the
enactment of several discriminatory laws against Chinese
Americans that were under consideration.

The Damage Caused by Exclusion

Exclusion did little to decrease Americans' prejudices against Chinese immigrants. In fact, prejudices and stereotypes flourished under exclusion because anti-Chinese groups gained legitimacy. In addition, Chinese Americans had little influence in a predominantly white society. Not only were fewer Chinese immigrating to the United States, but many were leaving as well. Chinese Americans were only .2 percent of the American population in 1880, but everyone was raving about "the Chinese question." By 1910, the figure was less than .07 percent. That meant there were fewer than seven Chinese Americans out of every 10,000 people in the United States.

In addition, most of those Chinese Americans were men. Very few Chinese women lived in the United States, and most of those who did were prostitutes kidnapped or sold by their families to work here. Chinese-American society was a bachelor society, in which men lived, worked, and socialized in groups. Few Chinese-American families existed at the turn of the century.

Anti-Chinese factions took advantage of the living situation of Chinese men and preached against the supposed evil doings of Chinese Americans. They made the Chinese out to be prostitutes and opium addicts, painting a picture of the illicit lives they led. Stories about the Chinatowns in San Francisco and New York surfaced in the first decades of the 20th century. One tall tale contended that there was a sinister underground city below San Francisco's Chinatown. The 1906 earthquake and fire proved this story wrong. Most of the stories and images of Chinatown were similarly concocted. Resourceful white businessmen in New York and San Francisco guided tourists through the cities' "menacing" Chinatowns, including on the tours visits to opium dens set up by the guides themselves.

Americans who had never even met a Chinese American had their impressions colored by articles in magazines and newspapers describing Chinese life and by a series of novels written between 1913 and 1950 about an evil Chinese villain. His name was Dr. Fu Manchu, and one book described him as having "the cruel cunning of an entire Eastern race . . . [with a] brow like Shakespeare and a face like Satan, a close-shaven skull, and long magnetic eyes of a true cat green." One of the only images of the Chinese in popular American fiction, Dr. Fu Manchu soon became a stereotype of Chinese people. Successful films in the 1930s brought the tales to life, casting Boris Karloff, an actor known for horror roles such as Frankenstein, as Fu Manchu. The American public could do little else but associate the character, and thus all Chinese, with the kind of nightmarish characters for which Karloff was famous.

At the same time, Americans were enjoying another movie series, this one centered around a Chinese detective, Charlie Chan. Though Chan was a "good" person, he still represented a stereotype of Chinese people rather than a realistic image. Americans were never given the opportunity to see what Chinese-American lifestyles were really like. One interesting note: Both Dr. Fu Manchu and Charlie Chan were played in the movies by whites made up to look Asian.

A small portion of the tales about life in Chinatown was based on truth. Chinatowns did have gambling parlors; in the bachelor society, there was little other entertainment. And secret associations, known as tongs, unofficially policed the neighborhoods. But the local police forces of the cities with Chinatowns were quite content to leave the job of protecting Chinese areas to the Chinese.

Chinese Americans During World War II

When the Japanese bombed Pearl Harbor in 1941, the United States and China became allies against a common enemy. Public opinion about Chinese Americans quickly changed.

As Americans tried to distinguish between Japanese Americans, who were being placed in internment camps, and Chinese Americans, new stereotypes about Chinese appeared. One article in *Time* magazine during the war was titled "How to Tell Your Friends from the Japs." The "friends" were Chinese Americans, and the article described the differences in appearance between them and Japanese Americans. The article included such tidbits as, "The Chinese expression is likely to be more placid, kindly, open; the Japanese more positive, dogmatic, arrogant." Now stereotypes favored the Chinese, but they were still stereotypes.

The Chinese still feared being mistaken for Japanese, which was quite dangerous in the United States during World War II. Fearing anti-Japanese violence, Chinese shop owners displayed signs in their windows stating THIS SHOP IS CHINESE-OWNED, and Chinese Americans wore buttons saying I AM CHINESE. They also lived in constant fear that they would be mistaken for Japanese and taken to internment camps.

Events of the time served to enhance Americans' new favorable view of Chinese Americans. In the spring of 1943, Madame Chiang Kai-shek, wife of the Kuomintang leader, toured the United

A song sheet picturing Lon Chaney as "Ching, Ching, Chinaman," ca. 1922. Racial stereotypes have been perpetuated by white performers made up in "yellow face" to portray Asian characters.

States. Thousands of Americans came out to greet her in every city she visited, and others followed her progress through extensive coverage in newspapers and newsreels at the movies. Americans saw a woman of grace and charm, dressed in stylish Western clothes and giving eloquent speeches. Educated in her youth in the United States, Madame Chiang presented a new, morally acceptable image of the Chinese woman. She soon became a heroine to many Americans.

With the new image Americans had of the Chinese, Congress realized that it could no longer justify excluding the people of a country with whom the United States was allied in the war. In addition, the Japanese had begun to spread propaganda that the Chinese had been mistreated in the United States. Taking into account the new image of Chinese Americans and hoping to counter the Japanese propaganda, President Franklin D. Roosevelt urged Congress "to be big enough to acknowledge our mistakes of the past" and to pass legislation to lift the ban on Chinese immigration. He noted that the repeal would serve to "correct a historic mistake." The bill passed easily, and Roosevelt signed it into law on December 17, 1943.

Chinese Americans needed no urging to participate in the war effort, however. Long before the ban on Chinese immigration was lifted, Chinese Americans spent thousands of dollars on the war bonds that helped pay the cost of the war. Urged on by feelings of patriotism to the United States and a sense of loyalty to China, Chinese-American men joined the armed services even before they had a chance to be drafted. All in all, over 12,000 men (or about 20 percent of Chinese Americans—a larger percentage than other ethnic groups because almost all Chinese Americans were men) served in the military during the war.

A New Wave of Immigration

After the war was over, a new wave of Chinese immigration began. But the immigrants coming to the United States in the late 1940s and later were not the poor laborers who had made up the face of Chinese immigration in the 19th century. Those fleeing from communism had more wealth and more education; the poor laborers remained in China, cheering the Communist victory.

This new class of immigrants wanted to settle in the suburbs, along with some of the second-generation Chinese Americans. These two groups were the new middle class Chinese Americans. But even though Americans felt a new warmth for them, the middle-class Chinese Americans who tried to move into suburban neighborhoods found themselves facing a large obstacle: prejudice.

In many neighborhoods, real-estate agents claimed houses were sold in order to keep Chinese Americans away. Others were bold enough to tell the Chinese Americans to their faces that they just weren't welcome.

Other Americans assumed that all Chinese were Communists, a devastating stigma to carry in the 1950s. They didn't realize that those in the United States were fleeing communism. But over the years, Chinese Americans persevered at work and in school. They excelled in many areas, and soon acquired a new reputation.

The "Model Minority"

Chinese Americans today have a mixed blessing. They are no longer considered evil, deceptive people. Instead, they are

New York's Chinese Hand Laundry Alliance marching in a demonstration to help the Chinese during the Sino-Japanese war of the 1930s.

counted as part of the "model minority," a phrase used since the mid-1980s to describe Asian Americans. Because Asian Americans as an ethnic group consistently rate higher in family income and education—they have the highest SAT scores of any racial or ethnic group in the country, including whites—they are praised for their hard work and productiveness. But lumping together all Asian Americans, or even all Chinese Americans, this way has proven to be a curse as well as an advantage and shows that Americans are not always sensitive to cultural differences between Chinese Americans and other Americans. For example, the average family income for Chinese Americans is higher than almost all other ethnic groups, even whites, because Chinese Americans more often have more than one wage earner in a family.

Sometimes these insensitivities are visible even when they

are masked by compliments. For example, saying that all Asians are good in school, particularly in math and science, Americans tend to put pressure on those Asians who are not so adept at these subjects. They are expected to do well and are ridiculed when they don't. Also, those Chinese Americans who are interested in other subjects besides math and science resent that people don't expect them to take to subjects like history or English.

This image of Asian Americans as great students has some-times hurt them when they apply to colleges. In 1985, the University of California at Berkeley as well as some Ivy League colleges like Princeton and Harvard were accused of setting quo-tas to keep Asian-American students out of those schools. Asians have been accepted to those schools at higher rates than their percentage of the population, and the quotas were supposedly established to keep their population within the student body consistent with their population in the country. But it is hard to justify rejecting Asian Americans whose SAT scores and grades are consistently higher than those of other Americans.

The schools accused insisted that they had set no such quo-tas. Princeton, for example, asserted that Asians were not accepted in the same proportion that they applied to the school because they were little represented among athletes and children of alumni, two groups that made up the majority of the student population. Berkeley, on the other hand, though it denied charges of discrimination, made a public apology in 1987 for the way it had handled the issue.

Chinese Americans do find some difficulty with college admissions because they tend to spend a lot more time studying than other students. This leaves little time for the extracurricular activities that college admissions boards favor so much. Many

Chinese Americans put pressure on themselves to do well in school, which in extreme cases can be threatening to their health.

And when Chinese Americans find themselves under too much pressure, they tend not to do anything about it. Studies have shown that Chinese Americans have low rates of mental illness, but this is probably because they tend not to seek professional help until the situation is urgent. As with the statistics on family income, the favorable reports from these studies are not reflecting something that Chinese Americans do better, just something done differently in their culture.

Racism against Asian Americans

Though many Americans consider Chinese Americans to be part of the "model minority," there are still those who discriminate against them simply because they look or sound different. Sometimes the discrimination comes from ignorance. For example, many American-born Asians complain that people will assume they don't speak English. They'll say, "You speak English very well," or, "You have hardly any accent!" Others will just speak loudly and slowly, thinking the Asian American will not understand otherwise.

Other discrimination, especially in the workplace, comes from a lack of confidence in Asian Americans. Though Chinese Americans are one of the best-educated ethnic groups in the country, they find themselves underrepresented among company executives. Some foreign-born Chinese Americans are kept in technical jobs where they have little contact with people, and they are seldom promoted to

 (continued on page 82)

Steve and Katy Cheng
Bucking Tradition

Steve and Katy Cheng are 19-year-old twins. They are both students at New York University.

Steve: Our parents came to New York in 1970. They were both professionals and already spoke some English. My mom's a radiologist at Mount Sinai Hospital and my dad is a pulmonary specialist. He's becoming pretty well known because he's combining some of the traditional Chinese medicine with Western medicine, which is cool. It's also trendy right now.

Katy: We grew up on the Upper East Side. Our parents gave us the best life they could provide. We never spent much time in Chinatown except to go to restaurants occasionally. My parents still love good Chinese food, especially the slow-cooked dishes from Shanghai. They own an apartment building in Chinatown which is, I guess, their main connection to the community. Steve and I don't speak Chinese.

Steve: It's kind of weird. Even though our parents don't *seem* traditional, they have pretty traditional ideas for our futures. They just assumed we would be professionals like most of their friends' kids.

Katy: There's just the two of us, Steve and me. So when we were little, Mom used to say we were double happiness and that twins brought great blessings on a house.

Steve: She doesn't say that anymore. Now we're like double trouble.

Katy: You see, Steve wants to be a musician, and I'm an artist.

Steve: We're both going to get degrees at NYU because that's what Mom and Dad want. I agree that an education will be an ultimate good. But I'm in a funk-rap band. I play guitar and write lyrics. The band is really my life. We call ourselves Open Door. Sometimes people think it's weird, a Chinese guy in a rap group. People just need to get over it. Music isn't about race.

Katy: I do mostly hand-painted photographs, but I also belong to this group of performance artists. I like being on stage and using my body as an art form. We deal with a lot of racial and ethnic issues in our pieces. I thought about going into theater when I was young, but I came to see that my roles would be pretty limited. A Chinese woman is still a Chinese woman, not just another American.

Steve: Really. I can see you in remakes of Charlie Chan movies now!

Katy: Although I would love to be in a Chinese movie like *Raise the Red Lantern.* It's pretty amazing that a movie that was so Chinese was popular in this country.

Steve: I think one of the reasons we both chose artistic fields is that it matters less who we are.

Katy: Our friends are of all races. Steve's girlfriend is from Puerto Rico. The guy I went to the movies with last night is white.

Steve: But we're starting to think more about our background than we once did. I mean, we feel like aliens in Chinatown.

Katy: Yeah. People speak to us in Chinese, and then when we don't understand, they kind of shun us. I think maybe one day I'll study the language. Like go to Taiwan for a year for an intensive or something.

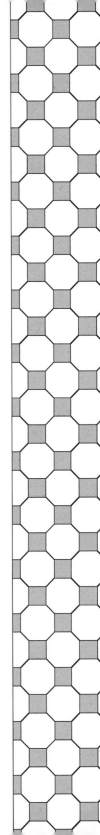

Steve: Not me. I'm an American. I have great respect for the Chinese culture, but why dig up things that aren't even a part of my past?

Katy: Sometimes we joke that we are mutant Chinese, you know, like the Ninja Turtles!

Steve: Boy, Mom and Dad hate it when we say stuff like that. It's not humor they understand.

Katy: I hope it doesn't sound like we don't appreciate all our parents have done for us. We really do. It's just a logical extension of having a good life that you want to explore who you are and what you want.

Steve: Actually, maybe one day they will see that we're a compliment to their lives and their efforts.

Katy: We're the new frontier, boldly going where no one has gone before!

Steve: Thanks a lot, Captain Picard!

executive positions. This phenomenon is sometimes called the "glass ceiling," the point beyond which even the most qualified Asian Americans are seldom promoted.

Sometimes the employees' speech and behavior can hinder their performance. Supervisors may cite language as a problem with foreign-born Chinese, but these same supervisors often fail to point out the problem to the employees. In addition, some experts say that cultural differences that cause Asian Americans to be more reserved and less aggressive and social at work can keep them from praising themselves and establishing the social contact that puts Americans at ease. The employees who have an ability to be friendly, easygoing, social, but assertive often get the first promotions.

The worst kind of prejudice against Asian Americans, however, is hate prejudice. Whites in all-white neighborhoods often object to the presence of Chinese Americans. One example was well reported in the 1980s. In Monterey Park, California, a suburb of Los Angeles, middle-class Chinese Americans—mostly immigrants from Taiwan—constituted 20 percent of the population. Resentful whites were known to display bumper stickers that said, "Will the last American leaving Monterey Park please bring the flag?" Obviously the supporters of this opinion did not consider Asian Americans to be American.

This kind of hate prejudice can sometimes turn violent. Chinese Americans are often attacked by anti-Asian and white supremacy groups. In 1982, Vincent Chin, a Chinese American, was beaten and killed in Detroit by two men who resented his tipping a white nightclub dancer. The two men who beat him were given a fine for violating his civil rights. They served no time in jail.

═ 5 ═

Lifestyles

The 19th-Century Immigrant

Τhe life of a Chinese American in the 1800s was not easy by any means. Whether as a miner, a railroad builder, a laundryman, or even a merchant, Chinese in the United States worked very hard for very little money. In gold mining, the only mines the white miners allowed them to work on were those the whites had already abandoned. On the railroad, they worked six days a week, sunup to sundown, for not much more than $1 a day.

In both lode mining and railroad construction, Chinese Americans worked for other people, but not directly for the companies. A Chinese American who spoke English well would act as a labor broker and gather a group of Chinese men to work together. The broker would cut a deal with the company for the entire group and then be in charge of distributing their wages. Similar brokers later provided strikebreakers during the many strikes of the 1870s.

But Chinese Americans in the 19th century were not just miners and railroad workers and factory strikebreakers. Many Chinese men worked at jobs that they never would have done in China—jobs considered women's work. As pioneers settled the West, few women came along at first. And women certainly didn't accompany the railroad crews through the Sierra Nevada range.

Chinese section,
Seattle,
ca. 1920.
Though Chinese
Americans often
worked with
other Americans,
they established
their own schools
and businesses.

So men had to take over the tasks normally reserved for women, such as cooking, laundry, and other domestic work.

The men who took on these jobs were mostly Chinese Americans. They opened laundries all over San Francisco, and they accompanied railroad crews and cattle drivers as cooks. They were hired by wealthy families to work as servants. It wasn't that they had these skills when they came to the United States; they learned them after they arrived here because these skills could provide them with wages.

Though they worked closely with other Americans, Chinese Americans didn't live with them. They settled in separate enclaves within each city and lived in totally separate societies. Chinatowns in San Francisco and Sacramento had their own schools and their own businesses, catering only to Chinese Americans—primarily because whites refused to allow them into their schools and stores. In fact, 28 states had laws segregating Chinese in school during the 19th century.

Sometimes this separation of societies was harmful to Chinese Americans, and they needed a representative to speak out for them and support their cause. A powerful Chinese-American group called the Chinese Consolidated Benevolent Association (CCBA) took on this role most of the time. Formed in the 1850s and commonly known as the Chinese Six Companies, the group acted as an advocate for fairness toward Chinese Americans and represented their interests to the white majority. The Six Companies was a powerful group composed of six Chinese district associations representing the Chinese of California. It controlled Chinatowns, acting as the unofficial government and police force. It also formed Chinese-language schools and fought vigorously against anti-Chinese laws. By the 1880s, the CCBA had branches in almost every other substantial Chinatown in the country. Even today, it still carries considerable weight in the Chinese American community.

The New Chinatowns

A lot has changed for Chinese Americans since the 19th century. Schools are no longer segregated, and whites and Chinese patronize each other's businesses. But life in 20th-century Chinatowns is similar in many ways to life for 19th-century Chinese Americans.

Since the resurgence of Chinese immigration after the 1965 immigration act, the number of foreign-born Chinese in the United

A bachelor
apartment in
New York City's
Chinatown. A
tiny room might
have housed
dozens of
undocumented
immigrants.

States has exploded. Half the Chinese Americans in this country are foreign-born, and a good number of them are poor Chinese. For these poor immigrants, particularly the undocumented immigrants, Chinatowns in the larger cities are their haven. Most of these immigrants do not speak English, but the tight-knit communities in areas such as San Francisco's or New York City's Chinatown provide them with enough Chinese-language services that they never have to learn English. In fact, immigrants in New York's Chinatown can go their whole lives without ever talking to a white person.

It's not that they don't want to learn English. But the majority of the populations of the largest Chinatowns—80 percent of New York's, 74 percent of San Francisco's, and 88 percent of Los Angeles's—are foreign-born. And these immigrants tend to work very hard and very long hours. Those who can find a few scant

hours to take language classes don't spend enough time in them to learn conversational English, and they don't have anyone with whom they can practice. Half the Chinese residents of New York's Chinatown speak little or no English. Without English, they are trapped in low-paying jobs.

Life for undocumented immigrants in New York City is very similar to the bachelor society of the 19th century and is typical of undocumented-Chinese-immigrant life in other big-city Chinatowns. Housed in the notorious tenements built before the turn of the century on the Lower East Side of Manhattan—where German, Irish, Italian, and Russian immigrants once lived—Chinese men are cramped into makeshift cubicles. The rooms are sometimes no bigger than five feet by ten feet, squeezing 50 people to a floor and 10 to each one-bedroom apartment. These *gong si fong* or "public rooms" are merely cubicles in illegally divided apartments, for which each immigrant might pay as much as $300 a month. The men who live in them work seven days a week, often at two jobs.

But unlike their 19th century counterparts, these men are able to save their money. Because they work long hours as waiters, peddlers, or construction workers; have no family with them; and have little spare time, they have nothing on which to spend their money except food and rent. Some use the extra money to pay off the $30,000 to $50,000 debt they owe to smugglers. Others have been able to save as much as $20,000 from their small salaries in just a few years.

For the undocumented families that come to New York, life isn't much different. They live in small apartments, and both parents work long hours to make ends meet. The women usually find jobs in the many illegal sweatshops operated throughout New

York's Chinatown. Though the Department of Labor regularly checks on conditions in the sweatshops, where hundreds of women sit slaving over sewing machines for up to 12 hours a day, they cannot always catch or correct some of the mistreatment the workers endure. Salaries are based on how many pieces of work the women complete each day, and many are forced to take work home or have their children help them (both of which are illegal) in order to make decent wages.

Company owners encourage this kind of behavior by tampering with the workers' time cards and making it look as though they make minimum wage, when they actually make much less. Since it became illegal in 1986 to hire undocumented workers, bosses have an advantage over immigrants, who know employers may ask about their immigration status. Owners use this advantage to avoid paying benefits like health insurance, social security, workers' compensation, or overtime pay for their workers.

Unions such as the International Ladies' Garment Workers' Union have tried to organize the seamstresses to help them get fair pay, but most of the women know there are many others waiting to take their places if they try to challenge the management. Furthermore, the undocumented immigrants are wary of joining organizations or letting anyone know who they are, for fear they will be found and deported.

Of course, there are others in the Chinatowns who don't live so poorly. But the majority of the people who live in the hearts of the original Chinatowns are recent immigrants, Cantonese speaking, mostly from Fujian (Fukien) Province. Those who have more money, speak Mandarin, and come from the northern provinces of China, or who were born in the United States, tend to live outside the original Chinatowns—in Flushing (Queens) and Brooklyn in

New York City, or in Monterey Park in California. Sometimes they own real estate in Chinatown, keeping the ties that their parents held when settling in the old neighborhoods even as they establish new ones in the modern suburban Chinese neighborhoods.

A Chinese-American woman at work in a sweatshop in New York City.

Chinese Associations

Chinese-American associations have long been a fixture of Chinatowns, helping early immigrants get jobs, find doctors, and settle disputes. Modern associations create gathering places for immigrants and help preserve Chinese culture.

There are three types of Chinese-American associations. The first are the family associations, also known as the clans. There are only about 100 surnames in Chinese, though they may be spelled many ways, depending on the Cantonese or Mandarin languages and the many dialects of each. The clans are based on the loose connection among people of the same surname. For example, one association might unite all Eng, Ng, Ong, and Woo family members, since they all share the same name in different languages and dialects. Family associations are traditionally service-oriented and were originally controlled by merchants.

The second type of association is the district association, or *huiguan*. Immigrants from the same districts or regions in China united to form unions of sorts. The *huiguans* helped the early immigrants find apartments and jobs, and lent money if a member needed a doctor. The district associations were also the ones who lent the first immigrants the money for passage to the United States, on the condition that they would work off the loans. The Six Companies was a union of *huiguans;* it had such control over Chinese Americans in the 19th century that it required anyone going back to China to pay a $3 departure tax and to settle all debts before leaving. It even convinced steamship lines not to take Chinese passengers who did not have certification that they had paid the tax.

The third type of association is often mistaken for all Chinese-American associations because it is the most infamous. Secret societies, known as tongs, have long been associated with crime and political rebellion. The first tongs in the United States were formed by Chinese Americans to oppose elite control by merchants. They profited through gambling, opium, and prostitution. But the tongs also provided medical care, lodging, and even death benefits for their members.

Through the 1960s, Chinese associations took care of their members well. But in that decade, critics began charging that the associations were hiding the appalling conditions in which Chinese Americans lived. Activists pointed out the social problems in the Chinese communities, such as sweatshop labor, suicide, gang violence, overcrowding, and high rates of mental illness. They charged that, though the associations were good at helping their members, they also perpetuated the inequality that existed between Chinese and white societies because they kept the Chinese from participating and assimilating.

These days, Chinese associations continue to provide services for Chinese Americans, though with less power than in the 1800s. However, the tongs have maintained their sinister reputation by running illegal gambling halls and associating with Chinese youth gangs. Some crime experts have even charged that an influential and wealthy Chinese mafia exists, whose control of organized crime rivals that of the well-known Italian mafia. Experts also worry that members of Hong Kong's 300-year-old organized crime groups, known as Triad societies, are moving their powerful operations to the United States in anticipation of Hong Kong's return to Chinese control, and that some Chinese-American tongs are already associated with the Triads.

Chinese-American Education

The residents of the new Chinatowns may not fit Americans' image of the "model minority," but their children often epitomize this stereotype by the time they complete their educations. Many struggling first-generation Chinese Americans resign themselves to a low standard of living, but they envision a better future for their children.

Encouraged by the Chinese cultural belief that all children can achieve good grades if they work hard, Chinese-American parents spur their children to study more and learn more than other students. This Chinese philosophy about the value of hard work differs from the American belief that poor grades reflect a deficiency in the child's ability or the teacher's methods, not an inadequate amount of time spent studying.

The myth of the "model minority" has its roots in the remarkable educational achievements of Asian Americans in general. The children of Chinese immigrants outperform most other ethnic groups in testing and grade point average. In addition, they lead the nation in number of hours spent on schoolwork. Chinese-American children study an average of 4.6 more hours per week than most American children.

There are several reasons why first- and second-generation Chinese Americans do better than other native-born students. Children of immigrants usually perform above average in school in general, and Chinese-American children are no exception. The children who are immigrants themselves have probably experienced time in Chinese classrooms, where students spend an average of 40.4 hours per week on academics (compared to 19.6 hours in the United States). Since half of the Chinese-Americans in the United States are recent immigrants, many of the Chinese-American students have experienced some amount of strict Chinese schooling.

In addition, the Chinese immigrants who have been admitted to this country legally, whether under strict exclusion or the more recently established preference systems, are the cream of the crop of China. The most-educated and the highest-achieving Chinese are encouraged to immigrate, and the poorest and least-educated find no place in the preference system. It is not a surprise, then, that children of these Chinese immigrants are achievers as well.

But even the children of poor, undocumented immigrants perform well in school, mainly because they are pushed very hard by their parents and because they want to save face. Saving face means not embarrassing oneself or losing the respect of others, and Asians are particularly sensitive to the concept of saving and losing face. Doing something to cause one's family to lose face is the greatest act of disrespect to the family and is avoided at all costs. Chinese-American students who don't perform well in school feel they have caused their families to lose face.

Religion and Philosophy

Saving face and having respect for the family are just two of the elements of Confucianism, a philosophy of behavior that has governed the lives of Chinese people since the second century B.C. Though it's more a philosophy than a religion, Confucianism has been the primary faith of Chinese since its adoption by the Han dynasty as China's official philosophy.

Confucius (K'ung-Fu-tzu) lived from 551 to 479 B.C., during the war-torn years of the Chou dynasty. As he watched the destruction that went on around him, Confucius tried to develop teachings that would restore order and harmony—a set of guidelines on how to live and govern. He based his philosophy on the idea that close, respectful relationships—such as parent and child, husband and wife, farmer and landowner—hold communities together. Those in power have a duty to set a good example by establishing and maintaining these relationships and teaching chil-

 (continued on page 96)

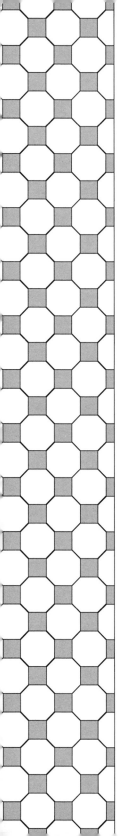

Arthur Fong
Speaking Out

*Arthur Fong is a 47-year-old political consultant who lives in
Los Angeles, California.*

I am a second-generation Chinese. I have always lived in Los Angeles, except for attending the University of California at Berkeley and graduate school at Yale. I was a good Chinese son until I went to college. Berkeley in the sixties was quite an experience. I did well academically, but my ideas of myself and my place in this country changed.

My mother and father are good, hardworking people who struggled to give me everything I have. But like so many people of their generation, they think hard work and a good education is the answer to everything. I don't think so. I see much in this country that disturbs me and I want to speak out and make it better. My parents think it best not to bring attention to oneself or to the Chinese community. They do not want to talk of the problems they have faced as minority participants in American society.

What is so interesting to me is that I want to talk about these issues and I am now paid a great deal of money to do so. I am a political consultant. I represent various Asian-American action groups. Community leaders, businesses, and elected officials want to know our problems and our opinions. We are a large and growing population on the West Coast and exert a certain political clout. Although I am Chinese, I see myself as part of a larger Asian-American population.

My parents are such a part of the Chinese community that they are only beginning to understand my role in representing a mixed Asian population. They still harbor resentments against the Japanese and Koreans. I tell them that we are no longer at war and that our similarities outweigh our differences. My sister, June, married a Korean man, Kim. They are both fine people. My sister is a writer of children's books and Kim is a noted architect. Yet to this day, both families are strained in dealing with each other. Of course, language is a problem for them all, too.

It is important that Asian Americans stand together, especially in a climate of growing violence. The incidence of hate crimes in this country is on the rise. Often an attack—either verbal or physical—against the Asian population is a "misdirected" one. For instance, if someone is mad at the Japanese about trade disputes, perhaps a Vietnamese will be harassed. Many whites can't tell one population from another. And many refuse to consider Asian people American, even if we were born here or have been granted citizenship. None of us, despite where we were born or if we have citizenship, are considered Americans. We are in this together.

When I am asked to speak to different community groups, I hear a lot of frustration from whites. On the one hand, they fear that illegal immigrants are going to overpopulate California and strain its resources. On the other hand, there is a resentment toward Asians because they do so well in school and in the marketplace. It is a no-win situation. Only by knowing the facts and seeing everyone as fellow Americans, regardless of skin color or accented speech, is there hope.

And despite my frustrations, I still feel hopeful. When I see my son and daughter in their school with friends and classmates from all races, I am cheered. They make friends so easily. My wife, Jin, immigrated to this country from Taiwan with her family in the sixties. She is a research assistant for an LA congressman. She has more perspective on this country than I do. Her idealism about the possibilities for a vibrant multicultural society buoys my faith.

I don't follow any religion, but the Buddhism of my parents has had an effect on me. I believe that if I practice right speech, right action, right intention, right livelihood, right effort—all parts of the Noble Eightfold Way—I will achieve each day a harmony that will further ultimate good.

This country is an experiment in the belief that all people can coexist with respect and tolerance for one another. I trust it will be a successful one.

Chinese-
American
Buddhists at
prayer. Most
Chinese
Americans,
including
Christians,
include some
Buddhist
elements in
their religious
practices.

dren about respect for age, tradition, and authority.

The result of these teachings was a philosophy that puts filial piety, or devotion of a child to a parent, at the forefront of Chinese behavior, along with a general ideology about proper conduct in all relationships. Confucianism takes on religious aspects when filial piety is extended to ancestor worship, a common practice among Chinese.

Up to the 20th century, Confucianism was China's official philosophy. But students in the Revolution of 1911 criticized old-fashioned Confucian ideals, and later the Communist government denounced Confucius as corrupt. Nevertheless, Chinese in all parts of the world live their lives by the Confucian code of behavior, which has recently experienced a resurgence in popularity.

There is no official religion in China, but Chinese still practice religious traditions that basically include elements of Confucianism along with the other two major religions in China, Taoism and

Buddhism. Taoism is based on the teachings of Lao-tzu, a Chinese philosopher from the sixth century B.C. Originally, Taoism encompassed a belief that through virtue and inward quiet a person can understand and live in harmony with *Tao,* the principles that underlie and govern the universe. Taoism combined with other faiths and traditions to form a sort of folk religion that is still practiced in many forms among Chinese and Chinese Americans today.

Buddhism had its origins in India, where the followers of Gautama Buddha (563–483 B.C.) started monasteries and religious pilgrimages. According to legend, Siddhartha Guatama, the son of a king of Nepal, was confined to his father's luxurious home because his father feared prophecies that his son would become either a universal monarch or a universal teacher and usurp his power. At the age of 29 Buddha had finally seen human suffering. He left his father's palace and wandered around meditating until he became enlightened under the Tree of Enlightenment.

He developed the Four Noble Truths, which explain suffering, including the path that leads to the end of pain, or nirvana. This path is explained in the Eightfold Path, a guide for proper behavior, which consists of right views, right thought, right speech, right action, right livelihood, right effort, right concentration, and right mindfulness.

Buddhism split into two basic forms about 2,000 years ago, and the Chinese now practice the more recent version of the religion. Chinese Americans have carried many Buddhist traditions with them to the United States, including marriage and funeral rites. For example, many stores in Chinatown sell the fake money that is burned at a Chinese Buddhist funeral to give the dead person's spirit something to spend in the afterlife. Chinese-American funerals often include burning incense and a great feast laid out before the coffin in case the spirit is hungry.

Chinese Women in the United States

One philosophical belief that has not really survived among the current Chinese immigrants is the Confucian view of women. According to Confucius, women had to practice the three obediences (to father when unmarried, to husband when married, and to son when widowed) and the four virtues (knowing one's place, not talking too much or at all, keeping one's appearance up for one's husband, and doing all the household chores willingly). Basically, Confucian beliefs kept women in a subservient position. Men even went so far as to bind the feet of noblewomen at a young age, supposedly to keep them dainty. Actually, the practice was brutal and painful, and only served to keep women immobile and dependent on men to get around (the practice ended with the Revolution of 1911). As late as the first half of the 20th century, many Chinese women in America with bound feet were confined to their small apartments, sentenced to a life of looking out the window because they had no means of getting around.

In the 19th century, the women who came to the United States were either prostitutes or wives and daughters of merchants. Few wives of laborers came because it was their duty to remain in China and take care of their husbands' families. Prostitution served to keep this split-family arrangement intact, since Chinese-American men formed few lasting relationships that would cause them to leave their wives. Prostitutes were usually either kidnapped or sold into the profession by their fathers to save them the expense of taking care of them. Then the prostitute's earnings became part of the family income.

Once Chinese women began immigrating in greater numbers after World War II, the role of Chinese-American women began to change. The new immigrants saw the lifestyles of American women, including marriage for love instead of by arrangement between families. Chinese-American women demanded the same rights for themselves. They gained much independence in the second half of the 20th century, attending college and holding jobs. Defying traditional Chinese roles, many Chinese-American women with the means today have college and graduate-school educations and work outside the home. They are doctors, lawyers, professors, accountants, scientists, artists, musicians, and practitioners of many other well-respected occupations.

Chinese-American Literature

One profession in which women have dominated among Chinese Americans is writing. Three of the most critically acclaimed Chinese-American writers are women, whose best-selling books have moved many readers and inspired a recent spate of Chinese-American writing.

Chinese-American authorship first produced notable books in the mid-20th century. Through such works as Jade Snow Wong's 1945 autobiography, *Fifth Chinese Daughter,* and Louis Chu's *Eat a Bowl of Tea* in 1961, Americans could step into the world of early-1900s Chinese Americans. But these early stories didn't capture much attention among non-Chinese.

Then, in 1976, Maxine Hong Kingston published a semiautobiographical book called *The Woman Warrior,* which won the National Book Critics Circle Award for best work of nonfiction.

The book tells Kingston's story of growing up biculturally in California in the 1950s and 1960s, relating the stories her mother had told her about her side of the family. Kingston followed up *The Woman Warrior* with *China Men* in 1980, another semiautobiographical book, this time about her father's side of the family. Kingston was noted for the storytelling methods she used, such as Chinese accents and writing that reflected the oral "talkstory" tradition in which she was raised.

Kingston opened many eyes to Chinese-American experiences and culture with *The Woman Warrior*, but no Chinese-American author made such an impression again until Amy Tan published *The Joy Luck Club* in 1989. The novel tells the story of four Chinese immigrant mothers and their four American-raised daughters. The book became a best-seller and spurred a new wave of confidence in Chinese-American authorship. In 1991, five new books by Chinese-American authors were published, including a new offering from Tan called *The Kitchen God's Wife*. All the 1991 books except Tan's center around the theme of growing up Chinese in the United States and coming to terms with the differences and similarities between Chinese and American cultures. *The Kitchen God's Wife* tells the compelling tale of the secrets a Chinese immigrant mother and her American-born daughter keep from each other because each thinks the other won't understand.

Political Involvement

Few Chinese Americans have ventured into the world of politics by running for public office. But their involvement in politics—as voters, campaign contributors, and political aides—is still important.

Historically, Chinese Americans have not had a political
experience in common. Until 1943, when the repeal of exclusion
gave Chinese immigrants the benefit of naturalization, they
couldn't even vote. Once able to vote, Chinese immigrants shied
away from joining the same party.

Instead, political loyalties among Chinese Americans have
tended to span a variety of political parties, from conservative to
left wing, with the majority registering independent. In fact, most
Chinese Americans dislike party politics because they have been
jaded by their experiences in China's political system. This
makes it more difficult to get Chinese-American candidates elected to office, since the Chinese-American vote is not concentrated
in one party. Even when they do support a single candidate, few
Chinese Americans actually go out and vote—they don't understand the political system, don't think they speak English well
enough (ballots can be translated into Chinese though), or just
aren't citizens.

Yet Chinese Americans are not shy about supporting causes
that are in their interest. They contribute a lot of money—from
across the country—to local politicians who are Asian or support
Asian causes. And they speak up on issues involving the treatment of Chinese Americans or Chinese abroad. In 1989, during
the protests in Tiananmen Square, Chinese Americans gathered in
front of the offices of the Embassy of the People's Republic of
China in Washington, D.C., and in New York, among other places,
to protest the military crackdown. In New York, they marched in
the pouring rain from the United Nations headquarters across
town to the Chinese Mission to the United Nations in an emotional
memorial to the slain protesters in China.

American politicians realized the importance of the support

Chinese-
American pro-
testers marching
on the United
Nations in June
1989. As many
as 18,000
people demon-
strated against
the massacre of
students at
Tiananmen
Square.

of Asian Americans long before such marches pointed out the power of this minority. The Asian vote is particularly important in presidential elections because Asians make up large portions of the populations in the states that carry the most electoral votes, particularly California and New York.

But Chinese Americans are only now uniting with other Asian-American groups to present a united political front on Asian issues. Differences over historic rivalries, such as with the Japanese over the Sino-Japanese War of the 1930s or with the Vietnamese over Vietnam's expulsion of ethnic Chinese in the 1970s, have kept Chinese Americans from merging their strengths with other groups for a common cause.

One way Chinese Americans are influencing politics is as political aides and consultants. Since aides are appointed and not elected, more Asians have been put into these highly influential positions than have been elected to office. Chinese Americans and other Asians have been instrumental in researching, drafting, and fighting from the inside for the passage of legislation that affects Asian Americans. In this way, they have even more power than those trying to influence politics from the outside. And many of these aides, analysts, advisers, researchers, and press secretaries are preparing to run for office themselves, using the knowledge they have acquired as political insiders.

The Craze for Chinese Food

Politics aside, one of the greatest changes Chinese Americans have made in American culture has been the introduction of Chinese food. When the Chinese first came to the United

States, they couldn't find anyone who could cook their food. So they opened their own restaurants.

All of these first restaurants served Cantonese-style food, since most of the immigrants were from Guangdong, where Guangzhou, or Canton, is the capital. But the cooks preparing the food were not Chinese-trained chefs—those professional men had no reason to immigrate to the United States. Instead, early restaurant cooks were men with no formal training in Chinese cooking. So their foods took on a unique American flavor.

Two of the most famous Chinese foods in the United States over the years were actually never made in China, but are distinctive American inventions. Chop suey was actually created in a San Francisco restaurant when the owner was faced with a hungry crowd of white miners who demanded dinner after hours. All the chef had were the leftover scraps from the night's dinner, so he stir-fried everything with a few Chinese spices and served up a historic dish.

Similarly, fortune cookies are not part of a traditional Chinese meal. They were probably invented in 1916 by a noodle-company owner in Los Angeles. While the Chinese have traditionally sent secret messages in cakes and cookies on special occasions, the idea of putting little bits of philosophy into the cookies is quite American.

Chinese food became extremely popular by the turn of the century, and restaurants spread across the country like wildfire. Soon it became chic to venture into the inner streets of San Francisco's or New York's Chinatown to spend an evening dining on Chinese food. By the 1950s, take-out food was all the rage, and Chinese take-out even popped up in towns that had no Chinese residents.

About that time, Chinese began arriving from other parts of China besides Guangdong in the south, and they brought other

styles of food with them. Hot foods from the west's Hunan and Sichuan (Szechuan) regions, slow-cooked dishes from Shanghai and Nanking in the east, and the light, noodle-based dishes from the north could be found in a variety of Chinese restaurants all over the country. Americans found a new interest in Chinese culture, spurred on by President Richard Nixon's visit to China in the early 1970s.

Today, Chinese food dominates the restaurant business, accounting for well over half a million restaurants in the country and serving every known variety of Chinese regional food.

The Port Arthur Restaurant, New York City, in the early 1900s. Venturing into Chinatown for an "authentic" Chinese meal was considered fashionable in the first half of the 20th century.

Chinese Celebrations with an American Twist

Food is central to Chinese-American holidays, particularly in the two that are most widely celebrated in the United States. Occurring at opposite ends of the year, the Chinese New Year and

(continued on page 108)

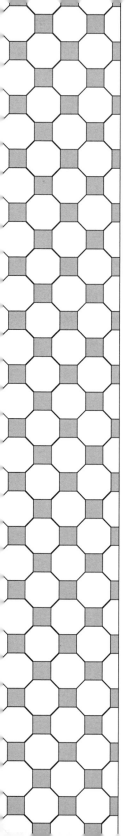

Ze Seng Dong
East Meets West

Ze Seng Dong is 53 years old and lives in Sacramento, California.
He is an acupuncturist.

Chinese people have lived in this area since the gold rush days, but I am a more recent immigrant. I came to the United States in the late 1960s as an engineer. I had a good job with an aircraft company in Los Angeles for a few years, but then was laid off with 65 other engineers. It was nothing personal. I then found work at an air base outside of Sacramento for a short time. I was laid off again. I couldn't believe it. They gave us notice one morning, a paycheck that afternoon, and let us go.

I was pretty depressed and decided to drive to visit friends in San Francisco, an hour and a half away. What was I going to do? I was on the freeway listening to the radio when the news came on: California had passed a law making acupuncture legal. I couldn't believe it. I had studied acupuncture and herbology with my grandmother in China the whole time I was growing up. I loved it. It was like a gift from the heavens.

I made plans to return to China to study for a year. When I came back, I opened my office in Sacramento. At first, it was mainly for Chinese clients. But word quickly spread. Soon I had a very busy office, with patients from all walks of life. I make a good living and I am my own boss. And I am able to help many people with a natural and age-old tradition. I am lucky to be so satisfied.

I married late in life, at 40, so I have three young children. My wife is also from mainland China, so we have much in common. We like living in Sacramento. We like the hot summers and the not-too-cold winters. San Francisco's Chinatown is just a short trip away. We have a big house with a garden and good schools for our children. Mostly, life is very good for us.

We have decided to raise our children only speaking English. We do not want them to be made fun of the way we have been sometimes because of our speech. People can be unkind and imitate you or act as if you do not know how to do things because of your accent. We want our children to be full Americans. I know it will not be that easy because they will still be Chinese, but their chances will be better.

My wife, Yining, and I are very interested in the history of this area. Chinese mined gold; helped build the railroad from Sacramento to Promontory Point, Utah; worked in agriculture; and started many businesses. It wasn't an easy history. The discrimination the Chinese faced was enormous. Yet, we live now in a very nice neighborhood in Sacramento and rarely feel excluded. But we feel it is important to know our history and to pass this on to our children. You should never say, "It can't happen again." History helps us build a good, informed life.

We also collect Chinese pots. Many Chinese settlements along the Sacramento River and into the delta area were washed away by floods and the changing course of the river. Now and then, the pots left float up out of the river. They are becoming collectors' items. My wife and I buy them whenever we can. We even found one once! Before the children were born, we were canoeing down the Sacramento River, up near Colusa. It was a quiet, beautiful day. Yining looked over and saw a small brown object about to float past. She grabbed it. It was a rough, brown glazed pot with a small mouth—probably used to store soy sauce or other liquid. We couldn't believe it. It was as if history had just popped up from the bottom of the river and presented itself to us. It is our favorite object in our house.

My work is something like that to me, too. Every day I treat modern-day people—with their suits and their high-tech jobs—with the medicine from ancient times. The past pops up every day for me and heals people.

I think both medicine and history heal people.

Harvest Moon festivities showcase many of the culinary traditions and folklore of China.

The Chinese New Year is a celebration of the lunar new year, or the new year according to the moon's cycles. It is celebrated during the first new moon after January 21, so it can fall anywhere from the end of January through February 19. Each year is named after one of 12 animal signs in the Chinese calendar.

In the days before the New Year, Chinese Americans clean their homes vigorously because once the New Year begins, sweeping might brush out the good luck that has arrived with the holiday. They also attempt to pay off all debts and start the year with a clean slate.

Parades and exhibitions in the streets include lion and dragon dancers and exploding firecrackers, all meant to keep away evil spirits. In fact, San Francisco has a block-long dragon made in Hong Kong in 1976 just for the New Year's parade. In Los Angeles, week-long festivities include a two-hour parade with paper lions and ten-foot-tall figures of Chinese gods. In New York, the costumed revelers spill out onto the streets for several days around New Year's Day.

In all American Chinatowns, tourists might spy a few of the good-luck traditions followed by Chinese Americans. Doorways are adorned with spring onions to usher in the spring, and red envelopes filled with money are handed out for luck to children and unmarried relatives. Dancers bring luck to the businesses and homes they visit. And on the 15th day of the new year, there are Lantern Festival parades during which Chinese riddles hang from paper lanterns adorning the shops and doorways of Chinatown.

Tourists observing the New Year celebrations might also feast on some of the traditional good-luck foods. For example, dumplings are good luck on New Year's Day because *jiaozi*, the word for dumplings, sounds like *jiao shizi*, the phrase for the time

when the old year meets the new. Tangerines and oysters are lucky because their Chinese names sound like the Chinese phrases for *lucky* and *good business*.

The New Year isn't the only time Chinese Americans enjoy traditional foods. Moon cakes are the traditional treat of the Harvest Moon Festival. These cakes, filled with sweetened black beans and lotus seeds, pay tribute to the goddess Chang O, who lives in the moon.

Legend says that Chang O was married to an archer who saved the earth by shooting down nine of its ten suns. He was rewarded with the herb of immortality, which he shared with his wife. Now he governs the sun while she governs the moon.

The Chinese choose the 15th day of the 8th month of the

A woman showing her grandchildren the banners posted during the Chinese New Year. Hanging banners with proverbs is one of the traditions observed during this celebration.

=— *109* =—

Chinese lunar year (around September or October) for the center of the Harvest Moon Festival because the moon is at its farthest point from the earth and appears very round and brilliant. During the day, Chinese Americans revel in a holiday that has been compared to American Thanksgiving—a time when families come together, celebrate the harvest, count their blessings, and honor the dead. But during the evenings of the festival, only the women participate in the moon-watching festivities in honor of Chang O.

Chinese Americans have come a long way since the days when their customs and appearance were considered odd, exotic, or dangerous. These days, almost every American has tasted Chinese food, whether it's taken out or delivered or eaten at the restaurant. Who can deny that the Chinese have affected almost every American's life when two people greet, like Chinese laborers of the 19th century, with the phrase "Long time no see." And when there is turmoil in China, as in June of 1989, American voices unite in protest and demand fair treatment for Chinese—a far cry from the passage of exclusion laws a hundred years ago.

Chinese-American history and culture have affected American history and culture in so many ways that they can't be counted. But Chinese Americans are still mostly new immigrants, and the changes they will bring to this country are constantly evolving and certainly not complete.

For Further Reading

Chan, Sucheng. *Asian Americans: An Interpretive History.* Boston: Twayne Publishers, 1991.

Chen, Yuan-Tsung. *The Dragon's Village.* New York: Pantheon Books, 1980.

Cheng, Nien. *Life and Death in Shanghai.* New York: Grove Press, 1989.

Kingston, Maxine Hong. *China Men.* New York: Alfred A. Knopf, 1980.

———. *The Woman Warrior.* New York: Alfred A. Knopf, 1975.

Kinkead, Gwen. "A Reporter at Large: Chinatown—I." *The New Yorker,* June 10, 1991, pp. 45-69.

———. "A Reporter at Large: Chinatown—II." *The New Yorker,* June 17, 1991, pp. 56-84.

Lee, Marie G. *Finding My Voice.* Boston: Houghton Mifflin Company, 1992.

McCunn, Ruthanne Lum. *Chinese American Portraits.* San Francisco: Chronicle Books, 1988.

Melendy, H. Brett. *The Oriental Americans.* Boston: Twayne Publishers, 1972.

Scholastic Update. September 18, 1987, and September 18, 1992, issues devoted entirely to China.

Takaki, Ronald. *Strangers from a Different Shore.* New York: Penguin Books, 1989.

Tan, Amy. *The Joy Luck Club.* New York: Putnam Books, 1989.

———. *The Kitchen God's Wife.* New York: Putnam Books, 1991.

Tsai, Shih-Shan Henry. *The Chinese Experience in America.* Bloomington, Indiana: Indiana University Press, 1986.

Wong, Jade Snow. *Fifth Chinese Daughter.* New York: Harper & Row Publishers, 1950.

Yep, Laurence. *Child of the Owl.* New York: Dell Publishing, 1977.

———. *Dragonwings.* New York: Harper & Row Publishers, 1975.

Yung, Judy. *Chinese Women of America: A Pictorial History.* Seattle: University of Washington Press, 1986.

Index